MIRACLES IN MY LIFE

Rex Humbard's Own Story

MIRACLES IN MY LIFE

Rex Humbard's Own Story

by Rex Humbard

Fleming H. Revell Company
Old Tappan, New Jersey

Scripture references in this volume are from the *King James Version of the Bible.*

ISBN 0-8007-0494-0
Copyright © 1971 by Rex Humbard
Published by Fleming H. Revell Company
All Rights Reserved
Library of Congress Catalog Card Number: 70-175524
Printed in the United States of America

To Maude Aimee —
my beloved wife,
mother of our four
children,
faithful coworker for
thirty years in the
work of the Lord.

Preface

"If God had a tent like that, He'd have a crowd like that!" I said fiercely to myself, as I watched the crowd surge through the entrance of the Ringling Brothers' "Big Top."

Gingerly, I unwound my stiff legs from the fence rail on which I'd been perched since early morning, and let my tired body slip to the ground. I turned to watch the last stragglers hurry in, but there was no envy in my soul, for I knew that money was scarce and there were no dimes for a circus. Besides, my parents were strict, and even if we'd had the money, they'd never have allowed us kids to see the big show. I considered myself lucky to have been allowed to come, at dawn, to watch the elephants and roustabouts shout and strain and tug to raise the huge tent.

It had been a long, exciting, happy day, and now it was time to head toward home. But, the vast expanse of that huge umbrella—such a far cry from the ragged old tent my gospel-preaching parents used for some of our meetings—demanded one last, long look.

"If only . . ." I thought, as I turned and started down the hot and dusty Arkansas road, "if only we could get God's work out of the dingy back alleys and put it where it belongs."

Ever since that long ago, never-to-be-forgotten day, I've been trying to do just that, for the Lord deserves the best. If people are to find Jesus Christ—their only hope of salvation—if we are to do what God told us to do—to rescue the lost for Him—we have to put God on Main Street and take Him into our lives and our hearts.

REX HUMBARD

7

MIRACLES IN MY LIFE

Rex Humbard's Own Story

1

Train up a child in the way he should go: and when he is old, he will not depart from it.
Proverbs 22:6

"This is an unlucky day, and something might happen," my dad said on the day I was born—on the thirteenth of August, 1919, in Little Rock, Arkansas. "I had a few more qualms than most fathers of firstborns, believe me," Dad used to tell me, "because my old childhood superstitions cropped up, and I had a hard time shaking them. But my Christian belief won out," Dad always added, "and it turned out to be a lucky day instead, for your mother was up and about her work sooner than most, and you never had a sick day in your life." Mother and Dad named me Alpha Rex Emmanuel Humbard—the first name after my father.

I have never doubted God's touch on my life, for the first words I recall were the prayers of my parents. When I was only two days old, my mother took me in her arms and committed me to God's service. "Rex," she instructed, "you are God's child. You are to be used of the Lord and you are not to go off after the world. If you do, sooner or later you'll get into trouble. You are to stay close to God and listen to what God has to say and do what He tells you in His Word, from beginning to end."

Mother and Dad were both evangelists, back in the days when men of God lived by faith and showed it. Dad was born and brought up on a farm in White County, Arkansas, about sixty miles north of Little Rock. He was a poor, hard-working boy, who had little education and no religion. His family did not attend church, but one Sunday he slipped off to Sunday school with some neighbor youngsters and a Sunday-school teacher gave him a Bible. Dad read the Word of God every chance he got—in the fields when he paused for a few minutes, early in the morning, and at night. He went to several different churches from time to time, and it puzzled him that in each church he was told the others were wrong. But he continued to pray alone, and he read his Bible, especially John 14:6: ". . . I am the way, the truth, and the life. . . ." And, when he heard the command of God, "Take up thy cross and follow me," he vowed to work to save *all* people, not those of just one sect.

Born in Chillicothe, Missouri, my mother, Martha Bell Childers, lost her mother when she was only eight months old. Later, she, her father and five brothers and sisters traveled by covered wagon from Missouri to Arkansas. One night the family attended a meeting, held by a woman known as Mother Barnes. The Childers family was deeply touched by the testimony of this former Catholic who had never touched a Bible until she was twenty-seven years old, when she found Christ during the revival in a little Methodist church. Twelve-year-old Martha and her family (with the exception of one brother) yielded their hearts to Jesus Christ and pledged themselves to winning others for Him. Her father felt God's call to the ministry and he remained a great preacher until the day God called him home. Martha gave herself to the work of the ministry and traveled as an assistant to evangelist Mother Barnes until her own marriage.

Although Martha Bell Childers and Alpha E. Humbard barely spoke when they first met at a preaching convention in Eureka Springs, Arkansas, each knew that the other was God's choice for his life's partner. They were not to see each other again for a full year, but finally they were united in the Lord, and their years of service together brought joy and blessing.

Having a small baby with them didn't interfere with the preaching of the gospel. Each night they brought me to the service. When I was old enough to walk, a pallet was made up for me on the platform behind the piano, and I fell asleep to the gospel music and the thunderous preaching of my father. Discipline was strict, for during their years of travel, Dad and Mom had lived in the homes of others and they had observed how different parents brought up their children. Now they were determined that *their* children would not be spoiled. Before the service, my father would lay his fingers over my closing eyelids and say, "Now go to sleep and don't you move until after the service." The first two or three times I was a bit restless, but after that I uttered no protests, and Mom said many latecomers never suspected they had a child there.

Only once, when I was old enough to toddle around, did my behavior provide an object lesson for the congregation. It was at a big meeting in Webb City, Missouri, and my father was being pestered by a couple of little girls who ran in and out of the aisles during the service. Dad didn't want to hurt the feelings of the girls' parents, but he was eager to protect the spirit of his meetings, so he prayed to find the right way to handle a reprimand. Dad told it this way: "At that time, we were staying in the home of a couple who had an only child also, and that child was allowed to do just as she pleased. Rex was permitted to play with her during the day since they were both about the same age, but we kept a tight rein on him.

"One night, Rex was in his usual place behind the piano — supposedly asleep. During the preliminaries, I heard footsteps pattering across the stage. I looked around and here was this little girl. She ran over to Rex, punched him and then ran off, taunting him to chase her. Rex rose on one elbow and looked at her, then he looked over at me and subsided. As the song service progressed, I guess I forgot about him. Just before I began to preach, I heard four little feet, instead of two, running across the stage. Rex hadn't been able to stand it any longer and had taken out after her. I said to myself, 'Well Lord, perhaps this is my chance to preach on raising children right.' I picked up Rex, laid him across the pulpit and gave him a good spanking; then I set him down, and I didn't have to tell him where to go. He beat it back to the pallet, put his finger in his mouth, and went to sleep. That is the last time that ever happened. Then I took my text: 'Train up a child in the way he should go; and when he is old, he will not depart from it.' "

One of Mom's favorite stories was about the time I went to Hiram's Bluff—a well-known cliff near our tabernacle at Pangburn, Arkansas—with Brother Snider, a visiting preacher. I was only a little over two years old, so Mom clung tightly to my hand as we climbed out of the buggy and peered over the cliffs. But she released me, reluctantly, to let me scamper over to Brother Snider, when he called out, "Look out there, little Rex. What do you see?"

"A bluff."

"Yep, isn't that great?" Then he asked, "Youngster, who d'ya think made that bluff?"

Mom said I backed up and looked puzzled for a minute, apparently amazed at the ignorance of this man. Then I looked him right in the eye and declared loudly, "God said, 'Let there be bluff,' and there was bluff."

In their first pastorate, Mom and Dad received no salary; they lived "by faith on free-will offerings." They were always on the move, and never accumulated much of this world's goods. Once, when the children were small, Dad told Mom, "I used to yearn to be able to leave the youngsters something, but God spoke to me and said, 'I've not called you to build houses. I've called you to build character.' "

We always had a family altar in our home. From babyhood on, I was taught the story of the King of kings. We literally lived by faith; money wasn't plentiful in that part of the country, and food was scarce at times. Mom's standard response to the news that there was nothing to eat was, "Get out the pans and then we'll pray. God has never let us down yet." And He never did.

We were poor by men's standards, but we were rich in the presence of God. We knew how to take God at His Word. Mom and Dad preached Bible religion—the Bible as it is. They didn't try to change it or overemphasize one part and neglect another.

Later, when he and Mom toured the country, preaching the

gospel, Dad said, "We never represented any denomination or sect, but preached Christ and the old-fashioned gospel, helping to advance the Kingdom of God and glorifying the Lord." Thousands of souls were won for the Saviour as a result of that decision.

I was the oldest of six children. My sister Ruth was born a year and a half later, and was followed by Clement, Leona, Mary, and Juanita. During the twenty-five years my mother and father spent rearing us, they were continuously in gospel work. They traveled all over the United States and Canada, and Dad pioneered and built many churches. He was a simple, down-to-earth, old-fashioned country preacher. He believed the inspired Work of God and preached it with power. Mother had real faith. If one of us kids needed a pair of shoes, or if there was no food for the table (and there were a lot of times like that during the depression), Mom would go down the hall, close the door and start praying. Whenever we had a need, we always told her and, if she went to that bedroom to pray, we knew something would happen.

One of Mom's favorite stories was about those depression days: "One night during the depression, we landed in Hot Springs with eight cents in our pockets. A lady who was taking care of our children and cooking the meals to help out while we were in revivals, came to Brother Humbard and asked if there was any money for food for the children. He said, 'No.' She began to cry. 'What are we going to do for these precious children?' she asked me. I told her to think of what she wanted to feed them and then to get her pots and pans and put them on the stove. She looked at me strangely. I said, 'We'll trust God to fill those pots.'

"I went to my room and got on my knees before the Lord. While I was praying, an old farmer (who had never heard of the Humbards) was awakened in the middle of the night by a voice that told him to get up at the break of day, gather vegetables and groceries, 'not a few,' and take them to the old theater downtown where we were holding the meeting. The next morning he came walking into that theater with a load of vegetables and all kinds of groceries. He said, 'I don't know who you are but a voice told me to bring these to you.'

"We'll never forget the day that God filled those pots and gave us a great feast. On top of that, the farmer and his wife both came to our meetings, were saved, and began serving the Lord in the local church."

Although Mom did all her own work, she never missed more than a few night services in all those years with Dad, and she never failed to pray at least an hour each day. Both of my parents gave us the greatest heritage we could ever have — a heritage of sincere dedication to the Lord's work and a faith in God. They taught us to live for the Lord and to trust Him.

Dad believed in the old adage, "Idleness is the devil's workshop," and his prescription for his growing youngsters was a musical education. Dad had always loved music, and he felt the lack of musical training in his own ministry. To purchase new instruments was out of the question, but a pawn shop provided ones that Dad could afford, at a dollar down, a dollar a week — a mandolin each for the girls, a guitar for me, a banjo for Clement, and a piano accordion for Mom (which Ruth promptly took over and soon learned to play). Soon the house resounded with noise from every room. Now Mom and Dad *really* prayed — for a way to turn that cacophony into real music.

A few days later a man knocked on our door and introduced himself. "How do you do, preacher. My name's Oscar Chilton. I'm a bit down on my luck, and I thought you might help me out. I understand larger crowds come to your church than to any other in the county, and I want to get into some church with my family. I was a music teacher in Chicago. I'd play the music just for the privilege of announcing for some students. I need to get some work in order to get something to eat for my family."

Dad accepted the Lord's answer to his prayer, and that Sunday Mr. Chilton and his two children played for the singing. Five or six pupils responded with requests for music lessons after Mr. Chilton made his announcement. But, at the end of the service,

16

Dad discovered that Mr. Chilton had rented a house nearby for ten dollars a month and he was afraid he wouldn't be able to meet the payments immediately.

"I'll tell you what I'll do," Dad countered. "I have plenty of rooms here over the church, where my family is living. I'll give you and your family a place to live with all utilities furnished, if you'll agree to give my family music lessons."

The deal was agreeable and we all began to study music. The teacher was excellent—a real perfectionist—and Clement, Ruth and Leona worked hard. To those three it wasn't drudgery; it was fun. But I was thirteen, old enough to know that if I learned to play I'd have to play every night at church and I wasn't about to do that! I dragged along, making a pretense of interest, until the third lesson.

Mr. Chilton grew more and more nervous and impatient. Finally, he lost his temper completely and shouted to Dad, "I'm going to throw this boy and his guitar right out that window, if you don't get him out of here."

"Now, what's the matter here?" Dad asked, looking at me sternly.

"I can't teach him when he just sits there biting his fingernails and staring out the window," the music teacher steamed.

"Dad, none of the Humbards is musical," I protested. "I've been with you at those family reunions in Muncie, Indiana, and Cleveland, Tennessee. None of the Humbards is good at music. It's just not in a Humbard, that's all."

The silence was painful. Then Dad said slowly, "Well, it's in one of them."

"Who?" I inquired.

"You." And with that he got out a switch.

Three months later, when the teacher packed up his family and started off to Texas, Ruth, Leona and Clement had already reached the point where they could study profitably on their own, but my own proficiency left a great deal to be desired. Dad issued an ultimatum. "I'll give you just thirty days to learn to play that guitar well enough to join the others on the platform for the services."

Stubbornly, I let the days pass by without practicing, but soon the dreaded Sunday night arrived. The church was packed, and there I sat in the front row, guitar in hand, barely knowing one note from another. Perspiration rolled from my brow and down the back of my neck. That guitar felt like a load of cement; I couldn't play a note.

Then, one night, listening to a visiting evangelist preach, I knew God was speaking to me. Suddenly, it was all different. When the preacher gave the altar call and the music started, I felt a small voice calling me to go forward to claim Jesus Christ as my Saviour and Lord. I had been brought up in church; I went to services just about every night, and my folks were what most people would label "religious." But right then I knew I had to make my own decision; neither church nor my parents could determine my standing with God. I hesitated, but evidently the Lord knew I needed a little push, because a Christian woman stepped across the aisle to ask me quietly, "Are you saved?"

I walked down that aisle and knelt at the altar and opened my heart to Jesus Christ. Light flooded my soul and I became a new person—I really wanted to live for the Lord. In that moment, God took my shyness away and made me an extrovert. I started talking about Him and I haven't been able to stop since. From that night on, I was often the first one in our meetings to jump up and testify for the Lord, something that had always embarrassed me before. The Lord changed my heart and made me over.

When the next Sunday night came around, my attitude about music had changed. I watched the person beside me closely as he played; I took in everything he did, checking his fingers in each position on the guitar. The following week, I bought a chord book and practiced for hours, and by Sunday night I was beginning to plunk away a little. With heightened interest and concentration— which is what I'd been lacking all those weeks with the teacher— and with all the zeal of a brand-new Christian, I made up my mind to learn. The next day I trudged over to the local radio station to watch a band perform. Each day I learned my chords by watching them play and then trying the same techniques at home. At last Dad's prayers were answered!

Clem and the girls joined me for practice sessions, and we worked together until we sounded pretty good. I placed a music stand in front of us and we pretended it was a microphone. "We need to learn to be professional," I told them, and we pretended we were playing and singing for a radio audience.

Our zeal must have been hard to live with, but my folks never complained. Sometimes we practiced until 2:30 in the morning! And one night, Mom begged Dad to shoo the children to bed, so she could get some rest.

"No," responded my father. "We had too hard a time getting them started. I'm not going to do anything to interfere now."

The local radio station, KTHS, had a two-hour Saturday night program known as "The Saturday Night Jamboree," which originated from the City Auditorium in Hot Springs. One day I went down and talked with the station manager about letting the Humbard group appear for one number, and he agreed. That night fifteen different groups performed and we ended up playing one religious song. When the red light flashed off, indicating that the broadcast was over, several of the station personnel rushed up to scold us, insisting that religious music wasn't appropriate on that program. We were a little disheartened, but returned home and turned the matter over to the Lord. The next week, the station invited us to return. They received eighty-five letters, sixty-five of which specifically complimented the Humbard group and requested more religious numbers on return engagements. Soon we became a regular feature. Gradually, the program ran as much religious music as secular, and the title of the show was changed to "The Country Store." Eventually, we were given our own Saturday morning program over the same station.

Not long afterward, a talent scout from the "WLS Barn Dance" came to Hot Springs and offered the four of us one hundred dollars each a week, to appear on the program in Chicago, plus additional income for road shows. That was big money for those days.

"What would we have to do?" I asked, warily.

"Well, I guess you can play and sing what you've been doing here but, naturally, we'd expect some hillbilly and secular numbers mixed in. I've got to hand it to you kids. With that variety, you'll be a great road show unit."

Gravely, I explained that we were interested only in spreading the gospel through our music, so we'd have to turn the offer down. The man from Chicago seemed disgusted. "You'll never go anywhere without mixing it up," he said.

"Look, mister, more people like gospel music than you think," I argued. "I'm sure we'll get somewhere just singing gospel songs. The Lord isn't going to let us down."

That scout must have been impressed, because the next Sunday night I looked down and, much to my amazement, there he was in the second row of the church! After church he introduced himself to my father, saying that he just had to meet the parents of a boy who would refuse that kind of money because of a conviction in his own heart. "I admit this is the first church I've attended in over thirty years," he said. "You've got to have something here. I thought just about everybody put money first and everything else afterward these days."

During those years we were kept busy playing and singing, first for church services and radio programs, and eventually for local events and concerts. Everyone seemed to enjoy our music — perhaps because we believed sincerely in the message of Jesus Christ, and we loved to give out the stories of God's Word. Sometimes we found it difficult to sandwich school in between radio broadcasts and church meetings, but somehow the Lord worked it all out. In the summer, when school vacations rolled around, the whole family packed up and we traveled all over the country, holding meetings wherever the Spirit of God led us. Those were times of great blessing and abundant fruit for the Lord.

While we were in Hot Springs in January of 1939, we were invited by V. O. Stamps (of the Stamps-Baxter Music and Printing Company) to go to Dallas for a March of Dimes Benefit program for the president's birthday celebration. It was to be held in the auditorium at the State Fair Grounds of Dallas. Mr. Stamps had called in singers and musicians from all over the country for the special event, and we Humbards were delighted to be included in the invitation.

20

Our trip to Dallas for the benefit proved to be memorable in more ways than I realized at the time. I had already recognized God's guidance in opening up a new area of service — how tremendous that area was, I was to learn within the next few months — but I did not know that I would also meet someone who would affect my future.

2

And the Lord God said, It is not good that the man should be alone; I will make him an help meet for him. Genesis 2:18

I was standing backstage at the State Fairgrounds Auditorium that eventful night in 1939, when I felt that prickly sensation we all get when we realize that someone is staring at us. I glanced up and met the most penetrating gaze I had ever seen—coming from one of the most attractive girls I'd ever seen. I knew I had to meet her. Without stopping to think of what I'd say, I walked toward her, brushing by the other two girls with her (obviously, they were all members of a trio), and blurted out the first thing that came into my mind: "If you're not going onstage right away, would you mind keeping an eye on my baby sister while we sing our number?"

"I'll be glad to," she replied, and I steered her quickly over to three-year-old Juanita and dashed after my family who were going onstage. I breathed a sigh of relief—at least she'd be there when I returned!

As soon as our number was over, I tried to hurry back to her side, but it was crowded backstage, and I was waylaid by the dynamic pastor of Bethel Temple of Dallas, the Reverend Albert Ott. "Look, son," he began, "I was impressed with the talent of your group and particularly by your number, 'The Meeting in the Air.' What about appearing on our church radio program tomorrow morning?"

22

All the time he was talking, I was inching my way toward my improvised babysitter and, by the time I had agreed that we would appear, I had reached my goal. Once I was at her side, I was tongue-tied, but the Reverend Ott came to my rescue. "Oh," he said, "you already know Maude Aimee?"

"Well, not really," I stammered, "but I sure would like to."

"Maude Aimee Jones, this is Rex Humbard," Mr. Ott said. "And I'm delighted to tell you that Rex and his family may be joining our radio staff at Bethel Temple — that is, if I can persuade him!"

Then, turning to me, he said, "Maude Aimee and her family are parishioners of mine."

God works in mysterious ways!

When we arrived at the radio station the next morning, we found Mr. Ott and Mr. Stamps had been conferring, and they had agreed on a plan to keep the Humbard family busy in Dallas for the next thirteen months. (Actually, it turned out to be two full years.)

Brother Ott explained that as pastor of Bethel Temple — a church with more than a thousand on the Sunday-school roll — he had at least thirteen radio broadcasts each week. He suggested that we work in his church and appear on all broadcasts. At the same time, we could help Mr. Stamps with his radio schedule and appear in concerts and musical programs in a 500-mile radius of Dallas. What an offer for four naïve country kids! While we had been yearning to declare God's power and love in song and story, God had been arranging just that — beyond our greatest expectations.

Financial details were incidental to us; all we wanted was to gain experience and sing for the Lord. But God provided for our needs. The whole family was to work in the church and appear on the thirteen programs each week. In return, Mr. Ott offered us rooms in which to live, and $37.50 a week spending money. In addition, Mr. Stamps was to give us an additional $25.00 for each concert and — best of all — he would supply free music lessons for all of us in either of his two music schools.

Every obstacle to God's will for us seemed to be swept away. Adamson High School (in Dallas) even gave us special permission to arrive late each morning so we could appear on the morning broadcasts.

One month later, we returned to Dallas and began weeks and months that were jammed full of activities. Usually, we appeared on as many as twenty-eight radio broadcasts each week, and attended two Sunday services and one Wednesday service at Bethel Temple. Our musical studies and schoolwork were sandwiched in, and any free moments were taken up by trips of from fifty to five hundred miles, doing concerts for V. O. Stamps.

Several weeks after our arrival, I was invited to a church young people's Valentine party at the YWCA. As soon as I arrived, I spotted Maude Aimee and I made sure I got the seat next to her. During part of the program I serenaded her with the song, "I Want a Girl Just Like the Girl That Married Dear Old Dad." When she smiled, I felt exactly as I had the day back in Little Rock when I won the award for pole vaulting—I was on top of the world.

They say an Arkansas traveler is slow, and Maude Aimee soon discovered that I was no exception. It took me six months to arrive at a state of "officially" going together. She was fifteen and I was eighteen.

Somehow, amid all of my activities, I managed to get my high-school diploma that year. Before we went to Dallas I had completed all of my work but a few credits, so my Hot Springs high school read my name out at commencement and awarded me a blank diploma. My real diploma was presented by Adamson High in Dallas. But, even with the name "Rex Humbard" being announced at two commencements, I missed walking down the aisle in a gown and mortar board. I was with the Stamps quartet, miles away, playing before an audience of eight thousand people. Nothing was allowed to interfere with the Lord's work.

On the day I graduated, Maude Aimee presented me with a tie and shirt. Maude Aimee still has the tie—a bit tattered and torn, perhaps, but still a reminder of our excitement that night. Mrs. Maude Jones had been widowed when Maude Aimee was only fifteen months old and, as a consequence, she was perhaps more strict in guidance than she might have been had there been a father in the home. I made no attempt to mask my admiration for this old-fashioned Christian woman, who had reared her tiny daughter and fast-growing older son in the fear of the Lord. It was a great satisfaction to me the day she gave me permission to take Maude Aimee to her first football game at the Cotton Bowl. "Only because you're a fine Christian young man," Mrs. Jones told me.

I loved to listen to Maude Aimee's mother reminisce about the old days. She had named her daughter after evangelist Aimee Semple McPherson, praying earnestly that God would grant her little girl grace to love the Lord and zeal to become a soul winner. Fortunately, the Christian atmosphere of their home was heightened by visits from many ministers; almost every great man of God who came to that area for revivals came to the Jones house for dinner and conversation.

Maude Aimee found Christ as her personal Saviour at the age of six — a tribute to her mother's faithfulness and her attendance at a church where the gospel was so clearly preached even a child could understand. One Sunday night the Reverend Ott ended the service by asking if anyone present knew the Lord as Saviour and wanted to be baptized. Anyone who wanted was asked to come forward right then. God spoke to Maude Aimee's heart and she was ready to obey Him.

At an early age, Maude Aimee discovered that she had a voice — not just an ordinary one, but a voice that must be a gift from God. Her mother taught her that this blessing was also a responsibility. Consequently, at the age of five, Maude Aimee started to sing on the radio every Saturday — singing the story of Jesus. When she was eight, she began to sing at most of the Sunday church meetings and at nightly revival services whenever it was possible. As she grew older, her life differed greatly from her schoolmates; she found her happiness, not in attending shows and dances, but in serving the Lord with the gift God had bestowed. And there was plenty of opportunity at Bethel Temple — the largest Assembly of God church in the United States at that time.

When Maude Aimee reached sixteen, she went to work as a window dresser for women's fashions for a large department store in Dallas, and she continued there until we married.

25

I was probably the most enthusiastic suitor in all of Dallas. Each morning, as soon as I signed off the radio program, I'd call her and, at 4:15 each afternoon, I'd race to her house and stay 'til church. The courtship was hard on Maude Aimee's mother, for we were carefully chaperoned every minute — even out on dates.

V. O. Stamps saw us together a great deal because we appeared frequently on the same radio broadcasts. Once I overheard him comment, "Those two are just meant for each other." And that comment prodded me to come to a decision. On December 19, 1939, I popped the question.

"Maude Aimee," I began, "I need you for my life partner." Then, desperately, I added, "In fact, I've just got to have you."

Maude Aimee startled me with a simple reply, "OK, Rex."

On Christmas Eve, I showed up with a huge box, three feet square, beautifully giftwrapped. She unwrapped the first box, then the others — each one nested in the next — until she came to a tiny one, containing a note saying, "Look in the other box." Now, thoroughly puzzled, she glanced up just as I drew a jeweler's box out of my pocket. In it was her engagement ring.

As I placed it on her finger, we pledged our love to each other and to the Lord. Together, with Him, we felt nothing would ever go wrong.

3

And we know that all things work together for good to them that love God, to them who are the called according to his purpose. Romans 8:28

In His wisdom, the good Lord knows when we are ready to receive the blessings prepared for us. And the old saying, "The course of true love never runs smooth," was as true for us as for scores of others since the beginning of time.

Maude Aimee's mother and my parents were devoted to the Word of God and they lived by it. Consequently, they felt that marriage should never be entered into lightly and, since Maude Aimee was only seventeen years old and I twenty, we were considered too young to bear the great responsibilities of marriage. In talking it over with our parents, we decided it would be wise to wait and become more firmly established in our life's work — His service. We loved the Lord so much we wanted to put Him first in everything.

Shortly before we arrived at this decision, the Lord had opened a new work for the Humbard family in Little Rock, Arkansas. It meant a prolonged separation for Maude Aimee and me — a time to test our love and let it grow in maturity — and although it almost broke our hearts, we agreed to get along on letters and telephone calls for a year.

The day we left Dallas, I drove the first eighty-five miles in second gear, but my sympathetic family did not say a word. Tears misted my eyes all the way to Little Rock, knowing that each turn of the wheels took me farther from the love of my heart.

Months of loneliness followed and we both tried to fill the void with letters and phone calls. The postman who delivered Maude Aimee's mail had an extra load to carry those days. Many times at least half a dozen letters were postmarked Little Rock, Arkansas, and I remember one day I managed to write eight letters — one of which was twenty-five pages long.

I tried to fill my time by working long hours; I bought time from radio stations and then secured sponsors to reimburse us. Every morning, seven days a week, our group gave a live broadcast at 6:15, which was piped into Pine Bluff at 6:45, and into Hot Springs at 7:15. By 8 A.M., the rest of the children headed off to school and I busied myself with the mail and cleared up business details for our activities.

The mail response from our hour-long Thursday night broadcasts had been overwhelming. The program, running from 11 to 12 P.M., pulled mail from thirty-three states and Canada. At the same time, the Lord was blessing us with revival meetings, tent meetings and services in almost every church denomination in the city. In addition, every Tuesday night we drove sixty miles for a service in our old home church in Hot Springs. By this time, I had assumed the duties of master of ceremonies, and I managed the arrangements and took charge of altar calls — all of which gave me valuable experience and eventually showed that God had given me the ability to encourage people to come to the altar to make a decision to accept Jesus as Saviour.

The nationally known evangelist Jackie Burris began a four-week revival in Robinson Memorial Auditorium in January of 1941, and he urged the Humbards to play for the services. We played for thirty minutes before each meeting, and the response was so encouraging that Mr. Burris asked us to accompany him to his next meeting at Cadle Tabernacle in Indianapolis, Indiana (an auditorium with a capacity of 10,000).

"Even if it does mean being away from home longer than usual, it's a tremendous opportunity," I suggested to the others.

"And it's a privilege for you youngsters to be a part of such a great meeting," Dad encouraged. "You may as well tell him you'll go, Rex."

The thrilling experience lasted six weeks and the crowds were

28

so large, thousands were turned away. My admiration for Jackie Burris and, most of all, my praise to the Lord knew no bounds. When the meeting was over, we rejoined our parents back in Arkansas and picked up our radio and church ministry.

During these hectic months of work, I noticed that Maude Aimee's letters were coming less frequently. They dwindled to an occasional note and, by the end of the year, her letters had ceased entirely. Confusion and despair took over, but, gradually, my confidence returned; I was sure that the Lord had a purpose and that He would work it out, to His glory.

One day an imposing envelope arrived from Dallas. It contained an invitation to a dedication ceremony for a new church. My heart gave a leap. Dallas! I accepted the invitation immediately, and a few days later I headed for Dallas with a prayer in my heart. I knew something was going to happen. It had to. I was going to see Maude Aimee again.

Memories flashed through my mind—of her sparkle, her very aliveness. I relived our courtship days and my heartbreak at leaving Dallas. What was she doing? I wondered. How did she feel? Once again, my heart leaped with hope and I repeated these words over and over: "Lord, direct me. I know You'll never fail me. You, only You, know my future—and what You want, I want."

In Dallas, Maude Aimee was startled to learn that we were coming for the dedication. She was dating a young man, just as I had been dating other girls in recent months. When her boyfriend invited her to the dedication service, she accepted. She felt that when she saw me she'd realize that she didn't love me and her imagination had been playing tricks on her, or she'd know for sure that I *was* the right one.

I stood on the platform that night, and watched her being escorted down the aisle. I knew she was beautiful, but I had forgotten what a picture she made. All I could see was that bright red dress contrasted against her black hair and eyes. She had on some kind of a rose-trimmed, black straw bonnet, and I wondered why all women didn't wear things like that. I couldn't keep my eyes off of her. I wouldn't have missed her in a crowd of five million.

Normally, as master of ceremonies, I could be depended upon to keep things running smoothly, but that night I missed some cues, and even Dad could see I was preoccupied. One thing was clear in my mind: there could be no other girl for me—ever. When the service closed and I watched her leave with that young man, I thought I'd lost her.

I spent a restless night, doing more tossing and turning than sleeping—but I prayed, knowing that God has the power to do anything. That night, He assured me all over again that prayer changes things. I couldn't see the evidence right then, but I had His answer.

"To every thing there is a season, and a time to every purpose under the heaven" (Ecclesiastes 3:1). God must have felt that at last we were ready to receive this blessing from Him. When something comes too easily, sometimes we don't appreciate it or treasure it. This struggle—this heartache—made victory even more cherished.

I left Dallas, but three months afterwards, Maude Aimee's mother received a letter from *my* mother. Mom told her about our current meeting in Indianapolis, at Cadle Tabernacle, and invited Maude Aimee to come up for the last week of her vacation. Mom added that the family was very eager to have her visit and wanted her to sing for our meeting. Just when the two of them were reading that letter and discussing the wisdom of accepting, the telephone rang.

"Look, Maude Aimee," I started in immediately. "I've got something I've got to discuss with you." I stopped, remembering that Maude Aimee was not a girl who could be coaxed. If she wanted to do it, she said so, if not, she'd make that equally clear. She broke in on my thought before I could proceed.

"Rex, I'd like to come to Indianapolis to see you and your family. Will you tell your mother and thank her for the letter? I'll take the train tomorrow morning."

I hadn't needed to coax; the Lord was answering my prayers.

I met her train and took her on to Cadle Tabernacle just in time to introduce her to the audience and let her sing. Afterward, we returned to the railroad station to claim her luggage and, on the way home, I got to the point right away.

"Are you willing to take up where we left off—when we broke our engagement?"

If she was startled by my abruptness, she didn't show it. She surprised me by answering, "Yes, Rex, I am."

"Will you marry me now? I'm not going to take a chance of losing you again. Maude Aimee, marry me this week."

She smiled slowly. When the answer came, I could barely believe my ears.

"Yes, darling, this week."

I knew that Maude Aimee—like any other young girl—had looked forward to a big wedding, so I suggested we go back to Dallas and have the ceremony there. But Maude Aimee was too practical for that.

"Rex," she protested, "it would cost more than we can afford to go clear back to Texas. We don't have that kind of money—not even a quarter of what it would take for my dream wedding—so let's forget about all that."

"But, honey. . . ."

"No, Rex, I've made up my mind. I'd rather keep what money we have for things we'll need after we're married. Let's ask your dad to marry us in a simple little ceremony."

Our wedding was scheduled for the next Sunday night after the evening service. Dad was to officiate, and Ruth and Louis Davidson, my sister and her husband were to be our attendants. Because Maude Aimee's mother and brother couldn't possibly make the trip to Indianapolis at that time, we decided it would be best not to tell them of our plans until the wedding was over. I kept thinking Maude Aimee was mighty brave to face all this so far from home, and I wanted to do all I could to compensate for her small wedding.

I guess I must have sounded mysterious that Sunday night, August 2, 1942, when I made my announcement at the service: "Folks, there's going to be a wedding immediately after the close of the meeting. If there's anyone who wants to stay, you're welcome."

Perhaps curiosity was the key but, whatever the reason, the small wedding wound up being celebrated by over 8,500 people!

The auditorium was full when the wedding march began and Maude Aimee entered from the other side of the platform. She looked radiant — more beautiful than ever in her light blue dress — as she took her place beside me, and Dad led us in our marriage vows.

"Everybody loves a lover," must be true of Indiana people, for the night after the wedding, August 3rd — the final night of our meetings — Cadle Tabernacle was packed with an enthusiastic crowd. The people who had witnessed the wedding the night before were back, and along with them were hundreds of people who had heard about it and wanted to see the new bride and groom.

Word must have gotten around that in all the excitement of the ceremony the night before, I had neglected to kiss my bride. So I walked out on the platform and declared, "I've been told that in all the confusion last night, I forgot to perform one important duty. Since I expect to make this marriage last a lifetime, I certainly want to start it off right. So, I'll try to make amends. May I present the new Mrs. Rex Humbard?"

And, amid the blushes of my wife and the laughter of the crowd, I kissed my bride.

After that final service, I drove carefully out of the parking lot, trying to ignore the clanking of the tin cans tied to the car. My embarrassment increased as car after car pulled out behind us to follow us down the highway. Honking horns heralded our progress all the way down to the business section of town, but they became far less disturbing after I heard a police siren signal us to pull over to the curb. I brought the car to a halt, and a grinning policeman said, "What's the idea of driving without lights? It's a law around here that you use lights after dark." Then he waved us on, and Maude Aimee and I agreed Indianapolis was the friendliest town we'd ever seen!

Early Wednesday morning we made our way to South Bend, Indiana, where, for a brief time, we made our first home — a three-room apartment on the second floor of an old house. It was a modest little place, but it seemed like a palace; everything in South Bend seemed wonderful. Our meetings were unusually successful. We had crowds so large the streets had to be blocked off. People stood outside the tent and watched the service because they couldn't get inside.

One evening God blessed us in a most unusual way. As I was leading the singing, I heard a woman near the back of the tent shouting, "I can see! I can see!"

I stopped the music and asked her to explain what she meant. She came forward and gave her testimony. She'd been listening to the music and praying to herself—enjoying the service, even though she had been totally blind for over sixteen years. As the songs warmed her soul she said to the Lord, "Oh, Lord, if I could just see the Humbards—just see their faces."

Suddenly, her head still bowed after the prayer, she noticed the hymnbook in her hands and, looking up in the direction of the platform, she could see light. Finally the haze cleared, and she could see our faces. Her shout of rejoicing and excitement, "I can see!" brought praise to our hearts. How good God was!

Many people in the audience vouched for the story of her long years of blindness, and we were thrilled at this miracle right in our midst. Eventually we saw God bless that meeting by scores of lives becoming dedicated to Jesus Christ.

While we were in that area, we drove over to the Winona Lake Bible Conference grounds to meet two giants of the faith in service for the Lord who were carrying on the work started by Billy Sunday—Mrs. Billy Sunday and Homer Rodeheaver. It was a privilege to meet these saints of God and to build our own determination to serve the Lord with the same zeal.

Our meetings in South Bend closed after that fruitful month, and just before we left, Maude Aimee and I celebrated our first month's wedding anniversary. I decided to give my lovely young bride a set of silverware to make her feel as if she were a real homemaker. We went out to dinner and exchanged cards—the beginning of a wonderful tradition in our home. Ever since then, when the second of each month rolls around, we celebrate our marriage. We had many lean months when resources were scarce, but there was always a flower, a tiny gift, to show our love for each other and for the Lord for bringing us together. We feel today that this custom has made our marriage grow richer and brighter each year. I urge couples to observe a similar practice; if they do,

33

perhaps the boredom and dissatisfaction of their marriages will disappear.

That fall, as we drove to Elkhart, Indiana, we noticed that the air felt particularly chilly for September, but we soon forgot about it in the hurry of unloading and settling into a small apartment.

I worked with the other men to find a place for the tent and erect it. Late that night a freak winter storm hit Elkhart—a blizzard so strong it caved in the tent, and there was absolutely no chance of using it for the services the next night. We managed to arrange to hold services in a local church for the first three nights, and I trusted the Lord would lead us from there.

I hadn't been expecting cold weather that early and Maude Aimee and Leona watched me shiver around for three days, before they talked me into buying an overcoat. I was trying coats on when I felt a slap on the back. I twisted around to face Jack Burris. He explained that he'd been trailing us all over town to see if we'd go along with him to provide the music for his next big Oklahoma campaign in Tulsa.

Jackie could be very persuasive. "Rex, after all this searching for you, you owe me a *yes* answer. How about it?"

I was cautious. "Look, Jackie, we'd love to go, but Tulsa's over a thousand miles away. I guess we'd have to be there by Saturday night and there's hardly time for that. We're already set up here."

"You'll be able to make it. I need you, Rex," he pleaded.

We rushed home to repack what we'd just unpacked and before midnight, we were on our way. Hard driving brought us into Tulsa by late Saturday night and we tumbled into bed, weary, but confident that we were doing God's will. That was all that was necessary.

The meeting was wonderful and, midway through it, all of us were given three full days of free time. Our cup runneth over! Maude Aimee had been longing to visit her home (she'd never been away from her family before) and this supposed trip of one week had already stretched into three months. Her family had been urging her to come home for a few days so they could share in the wedding festivities.

To save time, we decided to fly. Neither of us had ever been on an airplane before, so we were thrilled. Our friends greeted us, en masse, at the Dallas Airport and whirled us away to a combination shower and wedding reception at Bethel Temple which was attended by over two hundred people. At last Maude Aimee got her three-tiered wedding cake, almost three months after the actual ceremony! She was equally excited about the lovely gifts. I described the hardships of traveling with so many belongings, but couldn't persuade her to leave anything behind.

"Now, honey," I tried to reason with her, "we'll never be able to wedge all that in."

"I love all these pretty things, Rex, and I'm going to enjoy them, even if I have to sit on them all the way across the country."

All the way back to Tulsa we marveled at how we'd managed to stretch the excitement and celebration of our hasty, but quiet wedding, over three full wonderful months.

Our meetings resumed and Maude Aimee, while delighting in her new gifts and trousseau, had to face the aggravation of travel-busy days. I'll never forget her first crisis in washing clothes.

Her new bridal finery was so precious she wouldn't entrust it to a commercial laundry, so it piled up until one evening, she put her new lingerie in the bathtub to soak with the intention of handwashing it as soon as we returned from church. We were invited out afterward, and it was early in the morning before we got back home. Maude Aimee groaned as she faced the wash and I talked her into waiting until the next morning before she tackled it.

The next day we had to rush to the radio station for our program, then to a public appearance at the Chamber of Commerce, which was followed by still more radio programs. Before we knew it, it was time for the evening service again. Maude Aimee was sure she'd be able to get to the washing that night after the service, but again her plans were foiled by Jack Burris who had scheduled an engagement for us after the meeting. Once again we arrived home past midnight, so tired we could barely move. Again, she looked at the clothes in the bathtub and promised herself she would take care of them first thing in the morning.

Sunshine greeted us when we awakened, and so did a peculiar odor. Tracing the smell to the bathtub, Maude Aimee discovered her bridal finery covered with black specks—time had run out and mildew had set in!

We closed the meeting in Tulsa and packed up to leave. Looking at our luggage, it was apparent that even a magician couldn't pack that much into one car, so I purchased a little two-wheeled trailer, and, with a lot of ingenuity, we managed to get everything loaded before we set out for Little Rock.

It was nearing the Christmas season—the leanest time of year, financially, for traveling evangelists. Everyone seems to be too busy getting ready for Christmas celebrations to have revival services. My wife had hoped to spend Christmas in Dallas, but we were scheduled to open a meeting on January first in Augusta, Georgia, over a thousand miles away, and it was my job to get there early enough to complete arrangements for radio time, newspaper publicity, city permits, personal workers, and ushers.

We decided to leave early and travel alone, spending Christmas on the road heading toward Augusta. We'd never had a honeymoon, so I decided to splurge a little on her Christmas gift. I began the trip by giving her a wrist watch. It was so unexpected that she was delighted and, for the next hundred miles, the time of day was more fascinating to her than the scenery along the road. We stopped at Chattanooga, Tennessee, and spent Christmas Eve on top of Lookout Mountain. Just before sundown, we gazed out in wonder at the seven states visible below. All I could think of was that my Lord owned all that—the world was His—and we shared its treasures as joint heirs with His Son.

That night we found lodging in a lovely tourist home at the top of the mountain, and the gracious lady of the house served us breakfast on Christmas morning before we set out for Georgia. We were so happy, we burst out singing as we drove. We were celebrating the miraculous birth of His Son, and our hearts were full of thanksgiving that the Lord had brought us together. Life was so much fun. Harder times were bound to come, but with God to lead us on, we felt nothing would be too hard.

4

Now therefore go, and I will be with thy mouth, and teach thee what thou shalt say. Exodus 4:12

We arrived in Augusta the day after Christmas, and I set to work making the final arrangements for our first meeting scheduled for New Year's Day and locating an apartment. During those war years, it was no easy task to find a place to live — especially in Augusta — but the Lord finally directed us to a brand-new garage apartment, in South Carolina just a few miles away.

Seeing broken families reunited is one of the greatest rewards connected with the Lord's work, and our meetings in Atlanta provided several opportunities. One man who came forward to claim Jesus Christ as his Saviour brought his wife and two of his three children several days later. But he was very concerned about Oliver, his one remaining son, who refused to come forward.

I, too, was burdened for Oliver and I spent a long time praying for him. One night, after the service, I spied the boy walking down the darkened hall, toward the exit. I hurried after him, and asked, "Oliver, aren't you ready to give your heart to the Lord?"

Tears rolled down Oliver's cheeks, as he admitted, "I've stood it as long as I can. I'm ready, Rex."

There, in that dim corridor, the lost sheep became God's child and returned to his family fold. And God, in His infinite goodness, not only rescued Oliver from sin, He led him into a life of service — today Oliver is out preaching the gospel!

Another night, a young man knelt at one end of the altar, and a young woman at the other. Both gave their hearts to the Saviour. As they rose, their eyes met, and they rushed into each other's arms. This young couple was already in the divorce courts, but that night God made them over and gave them a new life in Him and with each other.

Along with the joys of serving the Lord, a preacher also witnesses the heartaches of people who refuse to heed God's call and are forever lost. I felt an intense burden for such a man, during an altar call one night. "The Lord is speaking to a person here," I announced. "Someone is getting his last call to give his life to God. Whoever you may be, listen to me: if you don't give your life to God, now — tonight — you will never have the opportunity to do so!"

Many people streamed to the altar, but my burden would not lift. I waited as long as I could, then I walked down into the auditorium, until I came to a man standing near the aisle crying. I knew at once that this was the one to whom God was reaching out. I spoke to the man softly, pleading and telling him that God was speaking to him.

"Today is the day of salvation," I reminded.

But the man shook his head and muttered, "No . . . no, maybe I'll come tomorrow night . . . not tonight!"

Finally, God took the burden from me and I mounted the steps of the platform and closed the meeting, remembering God's words, given to the prophet Ezekiel: "Yet if thou warn the wicked, and he turn not from his wickedness, nor from his wicked way, he shall die in his iniquity; but thou hast delivered thy soul" (3:19).

That same night, a few blocks from the auditorium, an unknown man slipped out from behind a hedge and attacked this man who had refused God's last call. There, in the darkness, the assailant robbed him, slit his throat and left him to die. Lost for eternity!

In Augusta, and in our next revival in Greenville, South Carolina, I handled the business details for the group as usual — taking care of the advance work and advertising, preparing the personal workers and ushers, and acting as master of ceremonies. But I also did some preaching, and I loved to preach. As

Dad once said, "The more I preach, the more I want to preach!"

I hadn't time to get any formal training at a seminary, but I did gain experience under the greatest of all Teachers, the heavenly Father, and I felt the Holy Spirit leading me each time I opened the Word of God. Both my brother Clement and I preached one service each a week. We depended on God and He never let us down.

It was decided that I should be ordained. The ordination ceremony was held in the Gospel Tabernacle in Greenville, under the auspices of our home church of Hot Springs, and my license was presented through the International Ministerial Federation, an association of independent ministers. Being Reverend Rex Humbard seemed strange. I prayed that God's unction would be upon me, and that faithfulness to God would always go along with my title.

Like my father, I wasn't interested in denominational work; I wanted to preach the gospel according to God's holy Word and the dictates of my own conscience. I felt that all of us could meet at the foot of the cross of Jesus Christ. And, like Paul, I wanted to be able to say, "And I, brethren, when I came to you, came not with excellency of speech or of wisdom, declaring unto you the testimony of God. For I determined not to know any thing among you, save Jesus Christ, and him crucified . . . And my speech and my preaching was not with enticing words of man's wisdom, but in demonstration of the Spirit and of power: That your faith should not stand in the wisdom of men, but in the power of God" (1 Corinthians 2:1, 2; 4, 5).

Often, in preparing my weekly sermon, I chose a Bible story to illustrate a great Bible truth, and many people told me that my method made the Bible clearer to them. I could not help but think, "Just as the parables of the Son of God did, two thousand years ago."

Crowds flocked to our meetings in Greenville, and I praised God that scores of souls were saved and started on a Christian way of life. It was the first big revival that had been held in Greenville for many years.

Maude Aimee had been ill ever since we began our service in Augusta. Each day she had fought to keep going, and, finally, I made her see a doctor. The one she consulted suggested she go into a hospital for tests and X rays and, when he examined the results, he told her there was something wrong with her digestive tract; he prescribed more rest and a special diet. She tried to calm down, following his directions carefully, but she didn't seem to improve.

In Greenville, Maude Aimee decided to try another physician. This time, after an examination, the doctor greeted her with twinkling eyes.

"Mrs. Humbard, there's no serious trouble, unless you'd put a new member of the family in that category!"

We were both delighted with his news, and more than satisfied with the diagnosis of her condition! But Maude Aimee fretted about the rest ordered by the doctor. She felt she wasn't doing her part in the services.

"Rex, if I could learn to play an instrument like the rest of you, I'd be much happier, and more use to the Lord, too. I've sung ever since I can remember, but I'd love to be able to play along with the rest of you."

"Honey, you're supposed to take it easy," I protested.

"Well, I don't have to sit around and be completely idle. Rex, please buy me an instrument and teach me to play."

"Choose any instrument you want, honey," I said, secretly pleased.

That statement I lived to regret! Maude Aimee promptly chose the vibraharp, and I bravely went out and bought one.

Her voice was a natural gift, a bell-like, soaring soprano, and she knew how to use it instinctively. But, thanks for that went to God, not to training, for I discovered that my wife didn't know one note from another; she had learned all of her music by ear!

I asked her to accompany me to the church and, for about an hour, we worked on fundamental chords. This turned out to be the extent of her music lessons. While not exactly a virtuoso yet, she did manage to chime in with the rest of us that night. Before the week was out, she was able to play like a veteran.

The vibraharp added a great deal to the richness and harmony of the group, but I never let her forget that our enjoyment began only after it was installed!

Many times, as I lugged it into a service, I teased her. "Maude Aimee, why couldn't you have chosen a flute or a French horn? Then you could have carried it yourself!"

From Greenville, we went to Gastonia, North Carolina, and then on to Louisville, Kentucky—to the famous old tabernacle of Dr. Mordecai Ham—the man under whose ministry Billy Graham was converted.

The meeting in Louisville made it apparent that people were hungry for the old-time Word, told in the same, simple unrepetitious way of the preachers and the pioneer evangelist who had made the tabernacle famous. Scores of people poured down the aisles in answer to altar calls.

Maude Aimee wanted to be near her mother for the birth of our child, so she went on alone to Dallas, while I accompanied the rest of the family to Bowling Green, Kentucky. It was the first time we'd been separated since our marriage, and I worried about her a lot and yearned to be with her. She wrote often, telling me about all of her preparations for the baby and about old acquaintances, but I could tell that the time was passing as slowly for her as it was for me.

A week before the baby's scheduled appearance, I went to Dallas, but the baby seemed in no hurry, no matter how eager his parents. As the weeks passed, I tried to plan ahead. It was clear that it wasn't going to be quite so easy to pick up and move from now on, and lodgings would be harder to get with a baby in tow. All of the Humbards had been having more and more difficulty locating a place to stay—as evidenced by our fruitless search in August—and had contemplated the purchase of house trailers as a solution. The initial investment would take a lot of money, but we knew God would meet whatever need we had; He always had.

One afternoon, Maude Aimee and I set out to look at trailers. We hadn't searched long before she discovered a little, sixteen-foot one, which contained a living room, bedroom, and kitchen, complete with butane heat and cookstove. To most people, it might have seemed not much bigger than a postage stamp, but to us it looked like a home.

I was figuring out if the price was within our limit and determining the financial arrangements, when Maude Aimee nudged me and announced, "Our house will have to wait for something more important, Rex. I think it's time to start for the hospital."

I hurried her into the car and raced frantically to Florence Nightingale Hospital. There Maude Aimee was whisked away by the nurses and I was left to pace the floor, each moment expecting to be greeted with the news I'd looked forward to for weeks. But it was a long, long wait. At 5:55 the next morning, I was told I was the father of a chubby, ten-pound boy.

When I saw him, my heart swelled with praise to the Lord. God had given us just what we'd longed for — a healthy boy. He had black curly hair and deep brown eyes. Maude Aimee had prayed that her baby would have a cleft chin like his father's, and I guess God granted that and added the hooked nose characteristic of the Humbard family, as a bonus. I felt a little of what Abraham must have felt, when he looked upon his son. I prayed that God would use this little one for His glory and make him a child, and eventually a man, of whom the Lord would be proud.

Assured that Maude Aimee was doing well, I returned home to rest after my night's ordeal! Once rested, I resolved that my son was going to have his own home and all the comforts that I, with the help of my heavenly Father, could possibly provide, so I went down and purchased our first home on wheels. (Little did we realize that this little house trailer, and eventually others a little larger, would be our home for more than ten long years of traveling and preaching the gospel to everyone who would listen.)

Four days after the baby was born, we brought him home. I got to ride in the ambulance with Maude Aimee, and to hold my son all of the way to Mrs. Jones'. Once there, we lay Rex, Jr., on the same bed his mother had been born in, just a little over twenty years before. While Maude Aimee rested, I managed to hold the baby — off and on — for most of the day. I knew that the next day I would have to leave him for more than a month, and I wouldn't be able to hold him.

I had to get back to earning a living. I prayed that I'd be able to meet our needs, little realizing that God had worked things out for me in advance. When I rejoined the evangelistic party, they were on their way to Nashville, Tennessee. Once there, I went down to Radio Station WSIX to make arrangements for radio time. I was surprised to discover that my old friend Jack Woliver (who had given us our start in radio in Hot Springs) was now program director of WSIX. He scheduled us for two programs daily, free of charge, and offered to help us promote our meetings at the Dixie Auditorium.

Three weeks after we began broadcasting, Jack called me into his office and told me, regretfully, that management was canceling the broadcasts. "Lack of time," he explained. WSIX was carrying both Mutual and Blue Network programs, and I guessed that management had figured that we produced few listeners.

Both Jack and I knew differently, but how could we prove it to management? Hurriedly, we devised a plan. We printed a picture postcard of the Humbard family, and next day both morning and afternoon broadcasts offered the card free and postpaid to anyone writing to request it. That one day's announcement astonished the station, Jack Woliver, and the Humbards, too. In the first twelve hours, we received 4,982 pieces of mail! By the end of the day, the number soared to 8,200 requests. We kept on with both programs.

Because of this encouraging response and the tremendous help of Jack Woliver, we were able to secure five Mutual Network programs each week, on a sustaining basis, originating from Nashville, Tennessee, and Bowling Green, Kentucky. Later, when we left Nashville, the network canceled two of those programs, leaving us with only three each week.

A still, small voice kept prompting me to do something about the change in schedule. Long ago, I had learned to obey God's commands, so, without any specific plans and with very little money, I bought a train ticket to New York. I was not afraid of circumstances; the only thing I was afraid of was failing to heed God's directions.

5

And they went forth, and preached every where, the Lord working with them, and confirming the word with signs following. Mark 16:20

New York was big and noisy and confusing, but I was determined. I made appointments with Mutual executives and explained that I wanted coast-to-coast broadcasts, five days a week.

They turned me down flat, protesting that there were already too many religious broadcasts on Sunday, and no one wanted religious songs every day of the week.

"Look, son," they told me rather condescendingly, "you're lucky to have those three programs a week. Be happy with your luck!"

"It's not luck, sir, and I still want five days a week. I'll offer the programs to someone else."

They laughed. "Go ahead. But you'll be back. Those other networks won't even give you three days a week."

New York seemed like the loneliest place in the world, but I shook off discouragement. I knew Someone was with me guiding me every step of the way. The Lord had led me to New York for a good reason, and it wasn't to be turned down by Mutual Network! With full confidence that I was following God's plan, I went to the NBC Building in Rockefeller Center and asked to see the program director of the Blue Network.

"Which one? We have five."

I reached into my briefcase and, to my chagrin, discovered I didn't have my notes. I'd left them back in the hotel room. I stared at that receptionist, unable to remember the name of the man Jack Woliver had suggested I see. I asked for a list of program directors, thinking I'd recognize the correct name when I saw it, but none of the names looked familiar. Hurriedly, I picked the first name on the list.

"Charles Barry — I'd like to see Charles Barry, if I may."

I was ushered down a long carpeted corridor to Mr. Barry's office. I opened the door and began, "Mr. Barry, a mutual friend of ours, Jack Woliver of Nashville, Tennessee, told me to come to see you."

Mr. Barry looked at me and grinned. "I don't know Mr. Woliver from Adam, nor you from Eve! Sit down and tell me what you've got on your mind."

It was obvious I was in the wrong office, talking to the wrong man, but there wasn't anything to do but go ahead and try to sell him. I breathed a quick silent prayer and began to tell Mr. Barry about our program and my desire to have it go coast-to-coast, five days a week. I discovered that Mr. Barry had never heard of the Humbards! But he asked for a record, and I pulled one from my briefcase. Placing it on the turntable, I watched his face as he listened to the Humbard family sing "Christ Is Keeping My Soul," on our Okeh release by Columbia Records.

Switching the record back to the beginning, Mr. Barry picked up the receiver of his telephone and asked to speak to his commercial manager.

"Could we sell this?" He played the record through again. Then he put down the phone and turned to me. "What else do you do?" he asked abruptly.

"Well . . . I read poems," I replied.

"What kind?"

I quoted the poem "Flowers."

Mr. Barry stood up behind his desk and announced firmly, "I'll take it! I'll have a hard time selling my boss on the idea — he's the man you came here to see. If you'd gone into his office, he wouldn't even have listened. But I'm going to take it."

I knew then that though I had made a mistake, that mistake

had been prompted by the Lord; God had guided me right to that very office. God works in mysterious ways.

After my return to Nashville, Charles Barry called to hammer out the financial details. God hadn't warned me about big business, and since all of our broadcasts had been on a sustaining basis, I was at a complete loss. With the help of Jack Woliver, we finally agreed on a one-year contract at four hundred dollars a week.

When I put the phone down, I drew a deep breath and tried to still my shaking knees. God had led me through a great experience and had shown me plainly that everything works out smoothly if we follow His plan. The extra money would be a big help in buying the badly needed house trailers, cars, and equipment we wanted.

I returned to Dallas, hitched up the new house trailer, and set off for Little Rock with my wife and son. Mom was thrilled to see her new grandchild for the first time, and soon the four of us joined the rest of the family and headed for Columbus.

Our evening services capped off very full days. Each day, before the night meeting, we spent three to five hours at the radio station for rehearsals and actual broadcasts. Rex, Jr.'s, presence didn't hamper us at all; we carried him into the control room, and he seemed to thrive on all the noise and excitement.

From Columbus we went to Pittsburgh, Pennsylvania, where we held five weeks of meetings in Carnegie Auditorium before moving on to Cincinnati, Ohio. During our five weeks there, we held services in Emery Auditorium, and, although the city suffered one of the worst blizzards in its history, the 1,800 seat auditorium was filled night after night. We rejoiced that people were so hungry to hear the gospel they were willing to brave terrible snows.

In Huntington, West Virginia, Maude Aimee and I traded in our little trailer for a twenty-five-foot one, which gave us extra room for a nursery for our growing, active son. Then Maude Aimee and Rex, Jr., left for a brief visit to Dallas, while I went on to Akron, Ohio, for services in Central High School Auditorium and broadcasts originating from WAKR. My family rejoined me

46

to share in the good fellowship of the wonderful Christian people in Akron, and to see the tremendous encouragement from the Lord in those meetings. I felt great warmth for these people who listened eagerly to every word of the gospel message and went out to let God's presence show in their lives.

Because we were on the move almost constantly, we began to have tire trouble. (In those wartime days, gasoline rationing and inferior tires were our greatest concern.) I managed to locate a replacement for fifty dollars, but the next one cost sixty dollars, and it lasted only fifteen miles. I was pretty digusted and had to really hunt to find a third tire and tube for ninety dollars. Forty miles was the most I managed to wring out of that one before it blew. By this time, my financial situation was desperate; I'd even been forced to dig into tithe money to keep tires on the car and trailer. Just a few miles outside of Erie, Pennsylvania, my newest tire blew. I got out of the car. All was quiet. Finally, Maude Aimee got out to check on the delay, and was shocked to find me kneeling on the busy highway, oblivious to the stares of passing motorists. I was praying, "Oh, God, I'm sorry. I'll pay my tithes — I promise I'll pay my tithes!"

There was nothing to do but park the trailer by the side of the road and leave it until we could find tires. Although the trailer door had a faulty lock and the trailer remained there three full days, everything was safe when we returned. We left it in God's hands, and He watched over it.

In the days that followed, I got caught up on my tithe money, and from then on we had no more serious tire problems. It was a lesson I'll never forget. When I preached on tithing from that day forward, I preached from experience. I knew how disastrous it could be to hold back from God the part that belongs to Him. The Lord had shown me that if a person gives the Lord His due, the rest of his money will be sufficient for all his needs.

In Erie, a big storm tore our tent badly. Water poured through the holes until the ground inside the tent was flooded. We tried to dismiss the meeting and send the people home, but they refused to go. They huddled under their umbrellas, holding their feet off the ground as best they could. God was there, pouring down His blessings right along with the rain!

Our next meetings were held in a large auditorium in Battle Creek, Michigan, and crowds filled it each night. The highlight of our stay in Battle Creek was our visit to the Percy Jones Hospital. We held services in every room — preaching, singing, and praying with seriously injured servicemen. It was a God-given opportunity to expand our ministry to the armed forces beyond our shortwave broadcasts to the troops overseas.

The next nine days were spent in Jackson, Michigan, in snow piled so high we could scarcely open our trailer doors. After much prayer, we decided to head south. We knew it would be difficult to get enough gasoline, but God worked things out miraculously — even the strict rationing regulations — and we headed for Oklahoma, stopping off in Hot Springs for Christmas.

6

The steps of a good man are ordered by the Lord: and he delighteth in his way. Psalms 37:23

We had a wonderful Christmas in Hot Springs with family and old friends. The season was made especially happy because Wayne Jones, one of our childhood friends, was gloriously saved. Personable, fun-loving Wayne was brought up under the sound of our ministry, but he had never made a definite decision to claim Jesus Christ as his Saviour. He had gone to school with all of us and had been courting my sister Leona for a long time. We used to tease him about his devotion to "The Little Lamb," our nickname for gentle Leona.

Wayne loved flying, and he intended to make it his career. He became a flight instructor at Muskogee, Oklahoma, and was doing extremely well, advancing rapidly in his chosen field. Gradually, he got away from his early home training and the influence of his wonderful Christian mother. He resisted the efforts of a church that prayed for his soul, and began to drink and live like the other men with whom he worked.

That year, 1944, when we returned to Hot Springs for the holidays Wayne happened to come home, too. Still in love with Leona, he went to the services at church as the best way to see his girl — she didn't let anything interfere with serving the Lord. Wayne felt the burden of his sin, and, in one shattering moment, he knew he had to turn to God. Kneeling at the altar, he found his way to the Saviour and arose a radiant child of God.

That very day, his heart was changed. Wayne felt the call to the Lord's service. He could hardly believe what was happening to him. He walked around in a daze, muttering, "How can God use someone like me?" But he had no doubt that God had intervened. The Lord had not only ransomed his soul, He had claimed his life!

Before we left Hot Springs, Wayne and Leona became engaged. He returned to his base of operations in Muskogee, but this time things were different. When he was asked to fly over to Arkansas to bring back a case of liquor for a party, Wayne refused. The other men were stunned, but no amount of teasing or pleading altered Wayne's position, and it wasn't long before their ridicule turned to respect.

When we went to Tulsa for our next meeting, Wayne flew up each night to join us for the service. Distance was nothing to a pilot, and Wayne was drawn to Tulsa as effectively as a moth to a flame. Previously, Leona's presence had been the reason for his flashing smile in the front row, but it wasn't the whole cause now. Wayne was seeking more of God; he discovered he was hungry to know God's Word, to grow in wisdom and understanding of the gospel he'd neglected for so many years. Wayne gave his testimony frequently in those meetings, and everyone was thrilled at the change in his life.

During his visits, whenever there was time, Wayne took us flying. From a safe vantage point on the ground, I had often watched him perform breathtaking tricks in the air. Now, I asked him to try a few spins with me. He was delighted to comply. I saw him smile broadly as he went into a series of twists. As soon as the wild demonstration was ended, Wayne glanced back to see how I was taking it. I was pea green!

Despite that initiation, flying fascinated me, and I wondered if flying might not be the answer to arrangements for our meetings. When I traveled ahead and took care of all the advance work for the next meeting—advertising, radio programs, city permits, rentals, ushers and personal workers—I couldn't be on hand to close the present meeting. More and more we realized that doing a good job for the Lord depended on planning details carefully in advance. Attendance was growing, and responsibilities increasing.

I took the matter to the Lord. As with other problems, I had the assurance that the Lord was bringing about His plan: ". . . before they call, I will answer; and while they are yet speaking, I will hear" (Isaiah 65:24).

After we closed the Tulsa campaign, we moved to Muskogee for nightly services. Since our network programs were finished, we were a little less pressed for time, and Wayne was still stationed in Muskogee, I asked him to teach me to fly. Wayne was an enthusiastic flight instructor, and it didn't take long for me to complete my training and receive a pilot's license.

It was obvious that a plane would cost a lot more money than we had right then, but God had an answer to that problem, too. The government was selling off surplus planes at Muskogee, and Wayne's company serviced these planes to prepare them for licensing. I asked Wayne about purchasing one and before we left Muskogee in March of 1945, we had our own plane.

Following services in Fort Smith, we held a great meeting in our home church, the Gospel Temple in Hot Springs, and before we left in June, Leona and Wayne were married in a quiet, moving ceremony performed by the Reverend John Hendricks. Although none of us suspected it then, Mr. Hendricks was to become attached to the Humbard family himself, for eventually, he and Wayne's widowed mother were married!

While my radiant little sister Leona returned with her bridegroom to Muskogee to begin their new life together, the rest of us went on to Houston, Texas, for our next meeting. Although the meeting attracted enormous crowds and was blessed so abundantly by God that it was held over for six weeks, the absence of Wayne and Leona left us all a little dissatisfied. Something seemed wrong; none of us said much, but we all felt it.

After two weeks, I called Wayne and invited them to join our party—to travel with us permanently. Wayne hesitated a moment before replying and then said, "Rex, I'd like to, but what could I do? How could I be of use to you and the Lord?"

I was encouraged by his immediate question about serving the

Lord. Since I believed this was part of God's answer to my prayer for guidance, I explained, "Well, you can do the flying, and other things will open up. I feel God has a use for both of you here. He'll show us what He wants."

Our conversation left me optimistic—certain that God was moving. Yet, for Wayne, the actual difficult decision had still to be made. God seemed to be reminding him of the call to service he'd received when he'd been converted—a call he had never fully understood, or discussed with anyone else.

To join an evangelistic party involved a big financial sacrifice for Wayne and Leona. When his boss learned that Wayne was contemplating leaving, he offered Wayne more money; his company had no intention of losing such a good man. Wayne and Leona discussed the matter thoroughly. They prayed and God showed them that this change was His will, so they prepared to join us as soon as possible. Wayne and Leona didn't want to take the slightest chance of disobeying God.

Our great meeting in Houston finally closed, and we had no immediate pressing engagement. We were all tired and in need of a change. Clement and his new bride, Priscilla, seemed grateful that a short break in the schedule would make it possible for them to take a honeymoon. Leona and Wayne also anticipated getting off by themselves for a trip and, of course, Maude Aimee and I had never had a real wedding trip, either. This free time seemed a golden opportunity for all of us. Excitedly, we made our plans for separate vacations, each carefully avoiding mention of destination to the others.

Maude Aimee and I had always wanted to see Mexico City, but now, with the opportunity to go, my wife was torn between two desires. She didn't want to be separated from our eighteen-month-old son, but she knew it wouldn't be practical to take a toddler to Mexico. I knew how desperately she wanted to make the trip, so I left the decision to her. Finally, she decided that Rex, Jr. would be in good hands if her mother came to Houston to take care of him. Maude Aimee's enthusiasm waned, however, when the moment of departure actually arrived.

When we boarded the airplane, Maude Aimee was tear-stained. We settled in our seats, and she waved to little Rex, standing beside his grandmother. But as the plane moved down the field, her tears returned—noisily. Passengers glared at me. I realized they thought I was the cause of her heartbreak, and I tried to comfort her, but nothing I said seemed to help. I gave up and started to pray. Through her flood of tears, Maude Aimee began to notice the attitudes of the people around her, and she perked up a little. By the time we landed on the outskirts of Mexico City, she was her usual exuberant self.

The startling contrasts of this cosmopolitan city struck us forcibly. The exotic scenery and beautiful buildings in the heart of the city only heightened the tragedy of the appalling poverty for the empty hearts and souls that lodged there.

We had reservations at the lovely Lincoln Hotel (which had been open only a month), and I was busy registering when I heard Maude Aimee's amazed cry. There were Clement and Priscilla who had no idea we'd be anywhere near! As we laughed together, we noticed other familiar faces. The Reverend and Mrs. Albert Ott of Maude Aimee's church in Dallas, walked down the hall. We were delighted to learn that they were assigned to a room two doors away from ours. All of us had a grand time on that vacation, although we tried to give the newlyweds—Clement and Priscilla—as much privacy as possible.

Maude Aimee was ecstatic when we took the boat ride and were serenaded by gondoliers. She marveled at the profusion of brilliant flowers throughout the city and became even more excited when I took her to her first opera. It was worth the whole trip to know I'd made her happy. I thought she bore up admirably under the strain of separation from Rex, Jr.! A few days later, however, as we returned to Houston, Maude Aimee could barely wait for the miles to pass to get back to her boy.

Out on the road again, bound for Memphis, we were content to be back in the Lord's work. The rest had restored our vitality. Once we arrived in Memphis, we began to prepare for the four-week meeting in City Auditorium. When things were pretty well set, I decided to fly our own plane to Nashville, to do the advance work for our next meeting.

The night I was to return to Memphis, I was flying southwest, approaching the Tennessee Valley, when I ran into a storm.

Visibility was so low I was forced to turn back, altering my course to take me up into Kentucky around the edge of the storm and then back into Tennessee. By the time I had completed the maneuver, it was getting dark. I had no radio and no night lights, and not the vaguest idea of my location. All alone, high above the earth, I had only God to depend on. I kept flying south, praying every moment for guidance.

Suddenly, I saw a small, red, flashing light. I smiled for the first time in what seemed like ages. To me, it was God's flashlight. Turning the nose of the plane toward that tiny beacon, I flew straight at it, but before I could arrive at the source of the light, complete darkness fell. I'll never know how I missed the high tension wires or how I made the final approach to a field without landing lights, but—somehow—I managed.

I alighted from the plane, mighty thankful for that solid ground beneath me. Peering into that darkness, I realized I'd landed on what appeared to be an auxiliary field for commercial airlines. Approaching a tiny building at the corner of the field, I found a lone man on duty. He informed me that this field was a cross-point for several routes.

"I don't have a car here," he apologized, "so there's no transportation to get you into town until the relief man shows up around midnight. You're welcome to wait here."

"What's the nearest town?" I asked.

"Just a small place—Henderson, Tennessee," was his answer.

When I finally got to Henderson, there was no hotel, but after a few inquiries I finally managed to rent a room in a private home. Then I tried to call Memphis. The phone was dead; the storm had damaged the lines and service was completely cut off.

As I waited for the weather to clear and dawn to come, I kept thinking how lost I would have been without God's guidance. I thought about the many times we all run into storms so severe we get off the right track and miss the pathway we're supposed to follow. Yet God is always there. Jesus said, "I am the light of the world." He is always there waiting, always shining, always accessible—if we'll look to Him.

I pondered the love of God for me, and for all men, and I got down on my knees to praise the Lord for His deliverance. I could have crashed the plane and been lost in those mountains, never to return. Then I thought how—years before—He'd offered me another "airfield of mercy." In my sin and darkness, I had seen the beacon of Jesus Christ, and I had found the only way to safety and security man can ever know.

If I could live a million years, I knew I could never praise the Lord enough.

7

For our light affliction, which is but for a moment, worketh for us a far more exceeding and eternal weight of glory. Corinthians 4:17

The next Sunday afternoon we opened with a great service in Daytona Beach, Florida, and the blessing was repeated again that night.

At dawn Monday, we were awakened by loud pounding on our trailer door. Sleepily, I stumbled to open it to two tall policemen.

"Are you the Humbards?" one asked.

"Yes," I replied.

"The city auditorium has just burned—almost to the ground. We managed to save the tractor next to the building, but we couldn't get to the trailer. Everything inside the building is gone, too."

As he turned to go, his voice softened, "Sorry, mister—hope you didn't lose much."

It was a staggering blow. The trailer and the musical equipment within the building had been worth more than $14,000. None of it was covered by insurance. With sinking hearts, we drove out to view the ruins. All of the instruments so necessary to our ministry—instruments we'd collected for fourteen years—were gone.

Turning to our bewildered little group, I said, "Well, here's where we use the faith we preach. If we quote from Romans 8:28, '. . . all things work together for good to them that love God, to them who are the called according to his purpose,'—then we've got to believe it ourselves."

As I spoke to them, I was renewing my own trust in the Lord. Trying to stand a little straighter, I encouraged, "All right now, let's get busy."

And get busy we did. We had announced revival services, and revival services were what we were going to have—fire or no fire!

By the time our radio program went on the air that afternoon, we had secured permission to use the high-school auditorium. I mentioned on our broadcast that the meeting would open that night, as had been earlier announced. We had to sing without instruments for the radio program, so I added that we'd be grateful to anyone who could lend any musical instruments for a few days, until we could start to replace ours.

If we trust God at His Work, He works everything out to His glory. When the public heard our services were going to go on, crowds poured into the meeting. Many who might never have attended a revival meeting, visited out of curiosity, and could see that we practiced what we preached. And once they heard God's Word proclaimed, they became hungry to know the loving Saviour who could carry His children through trials victoriously.

That first Monday night three instruments were loaned to us—a guitar, a mandolin and a solovox. The Spirit of the Lord was evident in that service, and we played and sang as we never had before. We were anything but defeated. What was money, measured against the worth of a soul?

For three nights we held meetings in the high-school auditorium, and scores of people came to the altar at each service. Then, a local man suggested we use a tent he owned, and another person loaned us plush seats from an auditorium in town. We erected the tent on the ball field and began tent meetings.

Hardship struck again. During the early morning hours following our second service in the tent, one of Florida's vicious tropical storms smashed across Daytona Beach. Daylight came, and we rushed out to find the tent torn to shreds and the attractive plush seats ruined.

Undaunted, we moved back into the high school and went on

57

with our meetings. By this time, almost everyone in town and people in the surrounding areas had heard of our misfortunes. The crowds doubled and, before the meetings closed, we saw hundreds of lives changed by their surrender to Jesus Christ.

We moved to Miami where we discovered that the story of our loss had preceded us. The news stories attracted hundreds who would never have thought of attending under less publicized circumstances. We felt the blessing of God in a most unusual way. We started to buy instruments again, replacing the old ones one at a time. We knew the Lord would help us and He did. Our hearts were so full with the blessing of God that we echoed again: ". . . we know that all things work together for good to them that love God, to them who are the called according to his purpose."

Once again, Dallas became our stopping-off point. While we held services in Bethel Temple, we made preparations for our first West Coast tour. Because of gasoline restrictions, the war years had made such a trip impossible, but now we felt that God was calling us to go there.

We decided to sell our plane before we left. It had served us well, but we could use the money it would bring more than we could the plane itself. Traveling west, we planned to visit some of God's majestic scenes along the way — Carlsbad Caverns, the Grand Canyon, all of the beauties of nature that constantly reminded us of God's words: ". . . Eye hath not seen, nor ear heard, neither have entered into the heart of man, the things which God hath prepared for them that love Him" (1 Corinthians 2:9).

The first meeting on the West Coast was scheduled for Angeles Temple in Los Angeles. That building, seating more than 5,500, was packed to capacity; there wasn't even standing room. We were delighted that our southern-style music was going to be popular here. If we could attract people to the meetings, we knew that God would be able to speak to them, and He alone could convict their hearts and lead them to salvation.

It was in Los Angeles that we made our first four recordings for Sacred Records.

Our next stop was the playhouse within the Old San Gabriel Mission. And, night after night, one visitor surprised us — a priest, who seemed to have the time of his life singing along with the crowd. Our type of program was something new to the residents of this town, and they responded enthusiastically. We saw God's blessing abundantly outpoured.

Midway through the meetings, a politician stopped by to request the use of the auditorium for one night. He planned to confront a young lawyer in a debate on current political issues.

"You can have it if you pay the rent for that night," I stipulated, "on one condition. The Humbards will come to the debate, announce our meetings and play and sing for twenty minutes before the debate begins."

This seemed like a great opportunity to reach people not usually exposed to church services, and the California politician assented readily. We played and sang our gospel songs, made the announcement about our future services, and finished with more music. The two debaters were introduced—the political incumbent who had interviewed me earlier about the auditorium, and his opponent, a rising young lawyer running for Congress named Richard Milhous Nixon. Before the meeting was over, the handsome, youthful Nixon had thoroughly trounced his opponent.

I was interested to see the young debater go on to win that congressional election and then go to the nation's Capitol. Years later, on a trip to Washington, I encountered the vice-president during the Eisenhower administration; it was, of course, Richard Nixon. As we were introduced, I smiled and inquired, "Do you happen to remember participating in a debate at San Gabriel Playhouse years ago?"

Mr. Nixon's eyes twinkled. "Yes, and I couldn't possibly forget all those banjos and bottles and bells the Humbard family played!"

And when Mr. Nixon took the oath of office as president, I couldn't help recalling how I'd presented in song, the wonderful news of Jesus Christ at one of his first political rallies!

Long Beach, Riverside, San Bernardino, and Fresno were all scenes of great meetings in those months on the Coast. The weather was sunny and mild, and every bright morning we regretted not bringing along a tent. Finally, I went out and purchased a portable B-29 plane hangar, and we hauled it up to Bakersfield.

While we were erecting this peculiar looking tent, a man strolled over and asked, "What are you putting up—another Golden Gate Bridge?"

I chuckled. "No—a gospel tent."

The man laughed heartily. "You could get all the Christians in this town into the first two rows of seats in that place!"

"If that's true," I countered, "then this is just the place we're looking for—we want non-Christians who will listen to the Word of God."

The first night the place was packed; cars were parked everywhere. A state highway patrolman came in, complaining that cars were blocking the highway, so midway through the song service, I asked everyone to cooperate by moving their cars to clear the roads. The patrolman stayed a few moments to listen, returned to the road, and came back in a very short time. People had moved their cars as he'd instructed, but in doing so, they'd blocked him in. With good humor, he stayed and enjoyed the rest of the service with them.

Bakersfield could best be described in Biblical terminology—"ripe unto harvest." When we left there, we felt that many more hearts were trusting in the Saviour than when we'd first arrived.

We moved on to Pasadena, then back to Angeles Temple for a four-week revival service which drew gigantic crowds. Two days after the conclusion of that meeting, on August fifth, Maude Aimee was admitted to Queen of Angels Hospital, and we welcomed a nine-pound, ten-ounce baby boy into our family. We named him Don Raymond. His sunny disposition was apparent right from the very beginning. When he was three days old, I brought him and his mother back to the trailer and took on the jobs of nursemaid, cook, and bottlewasher. My early training in helping to raise one brother and four sisters came in mighty handy.

When Donnie was nine days old, he began to travel with us, getting initiated early into what would be normal routine for the next six years. We set up the tent in Pomona, California, and began services and, less than two weeks after the baby was born,

60

Maude Aimee joined us on the platform, singing once again. But it became evident that it was too early for her to resume such strenuous activity, for she contracted a bad cold. She became so ill the doctors insisted she be taken back to Los Angeles to be treated by the physician who had delivered the baby. Thankful for an invitation to a friend's home there, she recuperated for two weeks, and I managed to drive up every day to help her with the baby.

8

. . . but they that seek the Lord shall not want any good thing. **Psalm 34:10**

When my wife recovered from her illness and Don was four weeks old, we left for Portland, Oregon. On the way, another testing of the Lord occurred — Dad Humbard was badly injured in an automobile accident. He was hospitalized with a fractured hip, and advised that he would be confined for a long time. The doctors gave us very little encouragement that he'd ever walk again.

We didn't give up hope — even for one second — for we knew the great Physician, and we were sure that Dad Humbard would recover and walk again as erect as ever. With God, nothing is impossible.

With Dad in the hospital and Mom by his side, sudden readjustments had to be made. The Portland meeting was scheduled to open immediately. Up until now, Clement and I had rarely preached more than one service each a week. Wayne, too, had spoken only occasionally. Mother and Dad were the real backbone of the preaching ministry.

We prayed about it, knowing that the meetings must go on. The duties involved in a big campaign are numerous, and one of the greatest difficulties is limited time to study. God was giving us a tremendous test. I started to seek God as I never had before, and I plunged myself into this great new experience with the Lord.

Humanly speaking, the Portland meetings could easily have turned into a fiasco. Dad was suffering; the doctors held out little hope—and we found out that even preachers can grow discouraged! But God's work doesn't follow human patterns. The meetings began to glow with the presence of God. We had sought a closer walk with Him and God had met our need, as He always had. The sermons touched hearts. Men and women, boys and girls, repented of their sins and wept at the altar. Others brought their troubled minds and bodies to God, and we saw God heal. That Portland meeting gave us all new faith.

It was then, as we were praising God together, that Wayne revealed his inner thoughts to me. "I've never understood it," he marveled, "but I know what I'm called to do. God spoke to my heart and called me to be an assistant pastor to some great man of God. The Lord told me that the very day He saved me. If it hadn't been for that, I'd probably never have joined this evangelistic party. Surely God needs men to assist, just as much as He needs true men of God to lead."

Had we stopped to analyze our experiences, undoubtedly we would have seen that God was preparing us to be used in a greater way. Already, I had experienced a ministry of music, a thorough exposure to business details, a training in touching the public as a master of ceremonies, and, finally, the wonderful joy of preaching God's Word. But the Lord had more in store for me. Step by step, He led us forward toward future plans.

We closed that victorious meeting in Portland and drove to Seattle, where we opened in a church of Swedish and Norwegian people who were used to an entirely different style of music and preaching. We prayed about this matter and decided that God meant us to stick to our own individual southern style. It turned out to be a happy choice, for the novelty of our songs intrigued those Scandinavians, and the meeting became one of the most remarkable in the history of our campaigns.

Many longstanding church members had never known the true joy of salvation in Jesus Christ, and at every service, people hungry for a personal relationship with God made their way to the altar to seek His salvation. The first woman who came forward testified that she'd never heard of "being born again." Once she

63

found salvation through Christ, she couldn't rest until she convinced everyone she knew that he needed this marvelous spiritual rebirth. The church was packed every night. All standing room was taken. Eventually we had to turn people away because of lack of space.

While we were in Seattle, Mom Humbard rejoined us and did her share of the preaching. "One of the greatest meetings I believe I was ever in was in Seattle, Washington. While I was preaching, people all over that big church began falling from their seats onto their knees. They began seeking the Lord, and we had a wonderful revival," she said later.

Throughout the Northwest the meetings continued. From Seattle, we moved to Olympia, the state capitol of Washington, and then on to Northern California for a one-week meeting in a high school. We kept as close to Dad as possible, and we prayed for his recovery constantly. Soon, it became apparent our prayers were being answered. Dad had improved so noticeably that we felt it safe to leave the area, entrusting him to Mom's devoted care. We moved south, taking meetings down into California once again.

At the time of our sixth wedding anniversary, Maude Aimee and I were in Stockton, California. Midway through a tent meeting, it became possible to take two days off to visit San Francisco as part of our family celebration. We passed through Oakland, where the new Neighborhood Church so attracted me I stopped to read the bulletin board on the church lawn. It was the most beautiful church I'd ever seen.

Jokingly, I remarked, "Wouldn't it be great to hold one of our old-fashioned revival meetings in there? I'd love to preach the old-time religion in that spectacular modern setting!"

We went on to San Francisco, and after we'd closed the Stockton meeting, we traveled to Lodi, a community of 10,000 people (most of whom were in the vineyard business). Every night over five thousand attended—quite a record for a town that size.

One afternoon, several men walked up and introduced themselves.

"I'm Earl Sexauer, and this is my musical director," one gentleman began, as he pointed to the man beside him. "Here's my card.

We heard the Humbard family back in 1944, in Cleveland, when the Christian and Missionary Alliance National Conference was held in the Euclid Avenue Baptist Church. Remember, that big old structure built by John D. Rockefeller? You people played and sang for the convention and right then I said to myself, 'Someday, Earl, when we build our new church, it would be wonderful to have that family for our opening services!' Boy, I certainly didn't dream then that all our prayers for a new church would be answered this soon, and we'd happen to come together here. Rex, would you hold a meeting in our church right away?"

I read the card handed to me in amazement. It said, OAKLAND'S NEIGHBORHOOD CHURCH, THE CATHEDRAL OF TOMORROW.

The church, which had just been completed, had caused quite a stir all over the West Coast. It wasn't hard to make up my mind. "We'd like nothing better than to join you for the opening, Reverend Sexauer," I agreed enthusiastically.

I could hardly wait to see the inside of that magnificent structure. I wasn't disappointed, either. The meeting itself was one of our greatest revival meetings. As many as two hundred people came to the altar in one night. The building was crowded for each service, and night after night, God touched hearts and lives for His glory.

The church's famous Port-O'-Call attracted many servicemen in the Bay Area, and we participated in those meetings, also. Earl Sexauer was famous for his illustrated sermons and the unusual features of his auditorium were designed to enhance that ministry. This method was a favorite of mine, as well, but tent meetings are not easily adapted to the use of visual aids. One evening, when we announced that we would play twenty-eight cowbells, we were astonished to see the choir rise into the air on a hydraulic lift and another stage appear, on which cowbells and sleighbells were suspended artistically!

The friendship between Earl and me deepened. We shared experiences, participated in daily radio programs originating in his church, and joined in services connected with the Bay Area Youth for Christ.

After two weeks of services in Fresno, California—our last California meeting—we learned that Dad had recuperated sufficiently to journey back to Arkansas, so, with thankful hearts we started home.

The next months were busy ones. We held meetings in Oklahoma, Kansas, Missouri and Indiana. While we were in Detroit, Michigan, we heard the catchy tune, "Everybody Ought to Know," and used it as a theme song for a while.

But when we hit Cadle Tabernacle in Indianapolis, Indiana—where Maude Aimee and I had been married—the bottom of our world dropped out.

9

And ye shall seek me, and find me, when ye shall search for me with all your heart. Jeremiah 29:13

Rex, Jr., had always been a healthy child and, when he developed a cough, we attributed it to a summer cold brought on by swimming in Lake Michigan and treated it lightly. But when he began to have difficulty breathing at night, Maude Aimee and I became concerned and took him to a doctor.

Gravely, the physician gave us the news: two-thirds of our boy's lung was collapsed; Rex, Jr., was in an advanced stage of tuberculosis. He was to be put to bed immediately and given penicillin every two hours, day and night.

The boy's life was in the hands of God. All of our lives, we had depended on the Lord of hosts as our Sustainer, so naturally we turned to Him for help. We sought the Lord with all our hearts, but our son did not improve.

When it comes to praying for someone as close as your own child, fear enters in and faith sometimes needs a boost. Maude Aimee decided to call her brother in Fort Worth, Texas, and ask him to pray for our son, too.

"Why don't you get in touch with Oral Roberts?" he asked.

"Who is Oral Roberts? And where?" my wife asked. She was puzzled, but eager to go anywhere, do anything God wanted.

"A minister from Tulsa, Oklahoma, who had tuberculosis in his youth," her brother said. "His heart is particularly burdened

67

for anyone with the same affliction, and he tries to share with others his own faith that God can heal."

When we learned that Oral Roberts had a meeting scheduled in Mobile, Alabama, we asked the doctor if we could take the boy. "It is too far," the doctor advised. "I would suggest that he enter a sanitarium."

Both Maude Aimee and I dismissed that solution immediately. We were sure that God could heal our child, for had He not given the Scriptural command: "Is any sick among you? let him call for the elders of the church; and let them pray over him, anointing him with oil in the name of the Lord. And the prayer of faith shall save the sick, and the Lord shall raise him up . . ." (James 5:14, 15).

We convinced the doctor that we would take a leisurely trip to Mobile, stopping along the way to allow our son all the rest he needed, and finally—reluctantly—he agreed to let Rex, Jr., make the trip. When we arrived in Mobile, we went at once to the tent service. And, when we responded to Oral Roberts' invitation to all those who needed prayer, we discovered that Charles Jones— Maude Aimee's brother—had notified the evangelist of our coming. The minister prayed fervently for Maude Aimee and me, asking God to bless us as servants in the Lord's work, so our lives would continue to be dedicated to preaching the gospel. Then, placing a hand on Rex, Jr., he asked the Lord to heal him of tuberculosis.

At the end of the simple prayer, he turned to us and said, "Go now and don't worry. The Lord has done the job."

We accepted the answer in faith, and left rejoicing, thinking of the words God spoke to Jeremiah, "Behold, I am the Lord, the God of all flesh: is there anything too hard for me?" (32:27).

In the services that followed, we took advantage of the opportunity to "take in" instead of "giving out" continually, as we were in the habit of doing. Hearing God's Word brings refreshment to the mind and soul. Sometimes, even preachers grow weary when troubles pile up, and this period of time, given to hearing the gospel message and meditating on His blessings, brought comfort to our hearts.

Rex, Jr., stopped coughing immediately, and he seemed to

improve right before our eyes. We left for Miami shortly after the meetings, and four weeks later, we decided to take our son to a specialist. We knew he was well, but we wanted proof so our testimony would be complete. The doctor examined him thoroughly, then pronounced him in perfect health. When we showed him the earlier X rays, he shook his head in disbelief and ordered additional X rays, as well as a complete fluoroscopic examination, immediately.

When the results were in, the doctor said, "The child's lungs are as good as new. No scar tissue shows on either lung, and we can find no infection anywhere in his body."

In the next three months, Rex, Jr., gained forty-two pounds, more weight than most children his age normally gain in three years.

All during this personal crisis, we tried vainly to set up an itinerary of meetings for the next three years. We communicated with the International Auditorium Association of America and other independent auditoriums, asking each for three-week dates. But, out of hundreds of auditoriums, less than ten supplied encouraging dates, and some of these were for less than the three-week periods we needed.

The meetings were to be city-wide campaigns, so we wanted a neutral location, apart from any local church. We decided we would have to use a tent, and God made a good tent available— almost immediately! Oral Roberts had his tent up for sale in St. Petersburg; he was buying a new one. We bought his old one and had it sent by freight line to Daytona Beach, where we had a successful meeting—not like the tragic experience we'd had before.

It was now early fall—the time of tropical storms in Florida— and when we moved to Pensacola, there were nights we didn't know whether we could hold a meeting or not. Many nights, lashing winds and heavy rains ripped the tent badly. We would pull it down, sew it up, and rush to erect it in time for the evening service—all done in the pouring rain but, with the help of God, we never missed a service.

Our testings didn't end, for after the rain came cold weather.

People shuddered in the brisk temperatures, while we prayed that the warmth of the gospel message would make up for their physical discomfort.

Closing the Florida meetings, we headed for Dallas to spend Christmas with Maude Aimee's family. In January we moved east to Augusta for meetings, but it was really too cold there for a tent service, also. We persevered and were rewarded by seeing many souls saved; the ones who did come really meant business. They were determined to find the Lord, and God rewarded them for their zeal—He met them there.

But, out of shadow, the Lord leads us into His sunshine. Our next meeting was one of the greatest meetings we'd ever conducted. It looked as if a twenty-four-hour-a-day revival had broken out in Birmingham, Alabama. People kept coming to our door at all hours of the day or night, asking how to be saved and requesting baptism. Never before had we experienced such large scale outpourings of conviction, and we gladly stopped anything we were doing in order to pray for these people.

One night, during an altar call, I felt strange. I pleaded for still one more person to respond. Minutes passed, and with a heavy heart, I closed the meeting.

Five days later, at the Friday meeting, a brokenhearted woman stumbled to the altar and sobbed out a pathetic tale. She had been at the Sunday service, and when they were leaving, her husband turned to her and admitted, "That last call was for me!" Two days later that young man was killed. Now, his wife cried in her sorrow, telling me I had been right—someone had heard his last call. Pride and stubbornness are tools Satan uses to keep a soul from finding peace with God, but I explained to that woman that God offered comfort, and forgiveness for her own sin, and that Friday night she surrendered to Christ—the only One who can bring true balm to a suffering heart.

The Birmingham meetings were exceptionally well organized, due largely to the efforts of the Reverend Glenn V. Tingley, pastor of the Christian and Missionary Alliance Church. Both Mr. Tingley and I marveled at the way God managed to meet even the smallest details in the arrangements—for example, if only twenty-five workers were available to help with counseling, then no more than that number responded to the invitation. In addition, the meetings were so fruitful that we at last had enough money to buy our own tractors and trailers — something we had longed to do for some time because of the spiraling costs of freight crating and hauling.

God had a plan for our lives. As we worked to bring lost souls into His Kingdom, He was working in His season to bring that plan about.

10

And, behold, I am with thee, and will keep thee in all places whither thou goest, and will bring thee again into this land; for I will not leave thee, until I have done that which I have spoken to thee of. Genesis 28:15

We were in Owensboro, Kentucky, when premonition hit me. The meetings were a disappointment after the previous two thrilling ones, but we never allowed temporary discouragement to get us down and were looking forward to our next meeting in Covington, Kentucky.

No matter how hard I tried, I couldn't shake the sense of danger. It was like receiving a telegram from God. I decided I'd better fly to Covington to check the situation there. Everything seemed just fine. The tent site was good; city cooperation satisfactory; and radio arrangements were exceptionally agreeable.

I was on my way back to Owensboro, when I made up my mind. "We're extending this meeting another week," I told the family.

"Why?" they chorused.

I didn't know why; I had no words to explain the still small voice within me that warned of unknown peril ahead. We continued the meetings and on the third day, disaster struck Covington—a cyclone devastated the area. The tent and trailer grounds were torn up so badly the cyclone fences were leveled. Had our equipment been there, everything would have been demolished.

When the news reached me, I felt shock and sorrow for the people in Covington, but no surprise. I could only praise the Lord for leading us with that still small voice. Sometimes we're so busy telling God what we want, that we fail to remember His admonishment, "Be still and know that I am God," but this time He had made me listen.

It was in Owensboro, in the hills of Kentucky, that six-year-old Rex, Jr., started school, but he could attend only for two weeks because our next meeting was in Terre Haute, Indiana. There, again our eldest son got in two and a half weeks of classes before we moved on. He appeared to thrive in each town—in spite of his brief attendance. He made friends promptly, and his first report cards showed straight As. We breathed a sigh of relief; clearly God was taking care of what we had thought might be a problem.

In Terre Haute, we battled storms again, but had a good meeting. We headed south, but the temperatures in Jacksonville, Florida, were around twenty-eight degrees—much too chilly for sitting in a tent. We installed huge blowers to make the audience comfortable, but still wound up trying to play our instruments with gloved hands, all bundled up in coats.

Closing the Jacksonville meeting early, we headed for Texas. During the Christmas season there, we completed our plans for another series of meetings on the West Coast, beginning with a revival in Oakland's Neighborhood Church and proceeding up to Seattle, Washington, for dedicatory services of the brand new Calvary Temple.

Unfortunately, after Christmas, Rex, Jr., came down with chicken pox. We managed to get him in shape to make the trip west, but the day we arrived in Oakland, Donnie, too, broke out with it! People living in well-regulated, comfortable homes often bewail the misfortune of childhood diseases, but I'm sure they can't imagine what it's like coping with similar conditions out on the road. The trying days of recuperation finally passed, and the boys bounced back to health once more. Rex, Jr., even spent five days in Oakland schools before we were ready to leave.

But the minor annoyances pursued us to Portland. Rex, Jr., blossomed red again—this time with measles! It was only a short time before he passed them on to Donnie. Although traveling—even living—became much more difficult, we managed, and went

73

on to enjoy splendid services in Portland and Salem, Oregon, before we moved on to Seattle.

Just before we left Oakland, Cap Stabbert called me. I hadn't seen Cap, a well-known Seattle businessman, since a Youth for Christ meeting with Billy Graham in Seattle, some years ago.

"Rex, you'll never guess what I'm doing now," Cap said. He paused dramatically, "I'm sailing the waters of Alaska."

Cap then proceeded to give me a brief run-down on what had happened in the intervening years.

Willis Shank, director of the Youth for Christ movement in Seattle, had felt God's call to the mission field. He resigned his position, bought a boat and set off to Alaska to minister to the Indian tribes on the islands. In a few short months he'd built a church in Alaska, and went back to Seattle to finish arrangements for getting his boat up to Alaska.

On Shank's return to Alaska to dedicate his new church, the Northwest Airlines plane in which he was a passenger failed to clear the top of one of the mountains. It crashed in the wilderness and every occupant was killed. The rescue party found most of the passengers and crew mutilated beyond recognition. But, unmarked, one body lay yards from the wreckage, apart from the others. Nearby, the rescuers picked up an open Bible and read on the flyleaf: WILLIS SHANK. On the opposite page were the words: SAVED BY THE BLOOD OF THE CRUCIFIED ONE.

When news of the tragedy reached Cap, he mortgaged his home, sold his business, bought a boat—naming it the *Willis Shank*—and took off for Alaska.

"I have dedicated myself to continuing Willis's work," Cap said. "When I heard the Humbards were on the West Coast, I decided to ask you to come along with me. Your music and preaching would be a great blessing to the Indian tribes." He paused for a moment, then concluded, "This work is a true missionary venture. There is no financial support, though; you would have to bear your own expenses."

I thought for a few seconds. Recently, money had come in unusually well. Was the Alaskan trip the reason God had allowed us this little extra? Had He prepared the way so we could make this trip? Quickly, I gave Cap our answer, "OK, we'll go."

The following weeks were busy ones. We continued to carry on services, while we prepared for the six-week Alaskan tour. My wife was worn out from nursing the boys through their illnesses, and participating in the nightly services and daily broadcasts, but looking forward to the tour boosted her morale and stimulated both of us spiritually.

Our train to Vancouver had cleared customs and crossed the border into Canada, when I received a telegram from the boy driving our instrument truck. He was being held at the border until the owner signed for customs clearance. I rushed off the train, found a taxi, and tore back thirty miles to clear up the difficulty. Then I rode the truck on up to Vancouver, joined the others at the docks and, together we boarded the *Prince Ruppert* (owned by the Canadian Steamship Lines) to begin the first leg of our journey.

Cap Stabbert and his family met us in Ketchikan, the colorful Alaskan town where the *Willis Shank* was berthed. The first major chore was transferring our instruments and luggage to his ship, which was to be our home for the next five weeks. As we stowed the gear, Maude Aimee came in for considerable teasing. In the confusion of packing, her shoes had gotten mixed up with the instrument cases which were sealed by government order. Until we boarded the *Willis Shank,* she had been stuck for a week with only the shoes on her feet — naturally, the high-heeled, impractical kind!

The twelve people in our party joined the *Willis Shank* crew of nineteen. For maximum efficiency, it was necessary that each one on board do his part in caring for himself and the ship. The work was divided, and we drew lots for our assignments. Maude Aimee and I were given the task of dishwashing, and I discovered fast that washing dishes three times a day for thirty-one people is no easy job. It took two hours after each meal to finish up. By the end of the trip, we both agreed that if we never washed another dish in our lives, we'd probably still be ahead of most people in experience!

Our itinerary took us into the humblest villages on all of the little islands, holding afternoon services each day and traveling on to the next port for evening services. Occasionally, when we couldn't find an adequate auditorium, the meetings were held on shipboard. Many of the people who listened so intently had never heard the name of Jesus before! Although most of them were English-speaking, we used an interpreter when it was necessary. The Indians — young and old — delighted in the music, whether they could understand the words or not. Rex, Jr., had been wanting to play the cowbells for some time, so now we set them up for him. Soon, he learned to play them with considerable skill, and the people laughed happily at his little-boy antics.

The Indians listened to the sermons with quiet attention — almost with awe. Usually, an entire tribe attended the service, and one night more than one hundred people came forward to claim salvation in Jesus Christ.

In one town, we discovered there were only two Christians, and they were not permitted to worship in public; everyone else claimed to be a communist. Although we were not allowed to preach or tell them the wonderful news of Jesus' love, we all sang for about forty children who came on board. Our hearts were burdened for lost ones in that town, blinded by sin and determined to spread their godlessness.

In those weeks we ministered through much of Southern Alaska and Western Canada. After we reached our northernmost point, we sailed back down the coast toward Seattle, taking the instruments ashore in rowboats at each stop. Often, we had to wait until after midnight for the tide to change so the Indians could shove the boats out through the breakers. We had only one accident on the entire trip; a wave struck a boat and tossed Wayne's bass fiddle into the sea. Fortunately, it floated and we got it back quickly, without damage.

The six wonderful weeks ended. We stopped in Vancouver, British Columbia, for a Youth for Christ rally and then headed for Seattle. It had been a great trip. We'd seen souls saved, and we'd watched people who had never heard the gospel listen hungrily and ask for more.

We had seen the fulfillment of God's promise: "So shall my word be that goeth forth out of my mouth: it shall not return unto me void, but it shall accomplish that which I please, and it shall prosper in the thing whereto I sent it" (Isaiah 55:11).

76

11

Delight thyself also in the Lord; and he shall give thee the desires of thine heart. Commit thy way unto the Lord; trust also in him; and he shall bring it to pass. Psalms 37:4, 5

Our Alaskan trip made us newly aware of what God can do in areas where people are longing and pleading for spiritual food. Where churches are found on almost every corner, we sometimes fail to realize the privilege of hearing God's Word preached regularly, of having fellowship with other Christians. Too often, we forget the value of our freedom and opportunity. Perhaps, if we took advantage of the opportunities for God's work we'd see a greater harvest of souls. In services in Birmingham, Alabama, and Evansville, Indiana, we urged people to seek God first, to let their souls prosper—not just their businesses.

Spring had come, and South Bend, Indiana, was next on the agenda. One day when I was surveying a lot, I noticed another man surveying the very same lot. We started to talk, and I learned that he was an advance man for Ringling Brothers, Barnum and Bailey's "Greatest Show on Earth."

"My job," he explained, "is to check the lot, order hay for it if it happens to be muddy, and be sure all is clear for tomorrow's setup. Three other guys traveled up here before me to make the previous arrangements."

He glanced at me inquiringly and asked, "What department are you in—for your show?"

Laughing at his terminology, I replied, "All of them. I rent the lot, take out the permits, make the arrangements for electricity, transportation, advertising, radio broadcasts, and telephone lines for on-the-spot pickups; then I solicit the cooperation of the local ministerial association and arrange for ushers and personal workers to counsel with converts in our meetings. When the tent arrives, I help drive the stakes, stretch the canvas and build the platform. On opening night I'm behind the pulpit, acting as master of ceremonies."

As I talked, his eyes got bigger and bigger. Then he said, almost as if talking to himself, "One guy can't do all that!"

I chuckled and kicked the clump of dirt beside me. "Well, how can I explain it? . . . I guess I'm kind of like that bumble bee over there. The scientist examines it carefully—measures its wing spread, weighs it, and says, 'According to aeronautical rules, it can't fly.' But the bee doesn't know that. So he flies anyway." I went on to explain about the part God plays—the important part. He nodded when I finished.

"You know," he said slowly, "maybe you're the ones who have the 'Greatest Show on Earth.' "

The circus was due in South Bend shortly after we started the meeting. On the morning it arrived, I got up at four o'clock and went down to watch them set up. I was curious to see how they did it. Their tent looked gigantic. It was so much bigger than our "Gospel Big Top," I knew I'd learn a lot. I watched them hoist the tent and set up their expensive equipment. I thought again as I had so many years ago, "God's work shouldn't be second best to anything. The Lord's people should have the best. We ought to be able to worship in the finest tent money can buy."

For a long time we'd needed a new tent. Storms had damaged the one we had, and it had been mended and remended. I went home and contacted one of the biggest tent companies in Chicago and drove up to talk to them about the kind of tent I would like to have. Our present tent seated three thousand people, but I dreamed of one that would seat at least six thousand.

The tent men started to figure. They drew up blueprints and finally gave me the cost of the tent I'd described—twenty-one thousand dollars! That was a lot of money. I knew there was no use going into such an undertaking unless it was God's will. Before we left South Bend, I'd prayed about it a lot.

Usually, when something big faced us, we tried "putting out a fleece to God," as Gideon had done. In order to know for sure that God was in on this transaction, I told the Lord that if at least one thousand dollars was received in the Sunday-night service, I would take it as His will to go ahead, and we'd order the new tent—on faith.

That night I explained to the people gathered for the service that we were sorely in need of a new tent. I told them that I had put out a fleece to God. I didn't beg or plead, and I was careful not to mention the specific sum I'd prayed about. I asked them to put into the offering plates what God prompted them to give. When the offering was counted that night, it contained exactly $1,060. We ordered the tent.

Now we had a goal to work for. The down payment was $6,000, and that amount had to come in fast. We started to work hard on promotion. Friends in South Bend helped tremendously, and before we could believe it, God provided the total sum of the down payment, and we were one step nearer our brand new tent.

The South Bend meeting was memorable in another way, for I witnessed a heartbreaking—but triumphant—incident.

One day before the meetings were to start, we moved the trailers into the South Bend trailer camp which was to be our home for the next few weeks. Out from behind a shed popped a ragged, grubby, freckle-faced lad.

"Help ya, mister?" he asked brightly.

"Thanks, son, but I think you're much too small for this."

"Oh, no, sir," he protested, "I'm strong—I'm real strong."

He picked up the nearby blocks and hauled them into place to prove it.

"What's your name?" I asked, after admiring his efforts.

"Lloyd, sir. What's yours?"

"Rex Humbard."

"Rex . . . I've never known anyone named that before. Could I call you Rex? I'd like that."

"Go right ahead. I'd like that, too."

Lloyd had such a kind heart and warm disposition that we all became attached to him and, as he warmed to us, he revealed his tragic story. Young Lloyd had lost his mother, brother, and sister, when a train hit the car in which they were riding. Even before the accident, his homelife had been wretched; his parents were separated because his father couldn't let liquor alone. Now, after the death of most of his family, he lived with his dad in a beat-up old trailer at the edge of the trailer camp. He knew none of the luxuries of life and pitifully few of the necessities.

Lloyd managed to get enough money for food by mowing lawns, running errands, and doing odd jobs around the neighborhood. The joys in his life were meager, but when he saw us putting up our tent, his eyes grew bright.

"Rex, what would it cost me to come to your meeting in the tent? If I work real hard, maybe I could earn enough."

Those big, brown eyes reached right down to my heart. "It's free to everyone, Lloyd, you can come all you want—every night, if you wish. I'll have a special seat right down here in front, just for you."

From that first service on, little Lloyd's chair was never empty. He listened to the sermons eagerly and drank in the beauty of the music. One night, I watched him walk determinedly to the altar. He knew what it was all about; he wanted his sins forgiven; he wanted the Lord Jesus to save him.

From that night on, we noticed how hungry Lloyd was to learn more of the Word of God. I gave him a Bible for his very own, and he tucked it under his arm and carried it proudly into the service. He was only eleven years old, but his heart had been deeply touched. Never before had he known such happiness. The wistful, woebegone look disappeared; his smile became a beam. Lack of money, lack of love, would never again defeat him. Now, he had the love of God.

One day, as I was going into a drugstore to place a long distance call, Lloyd rode by on his old bike.

"Hi, Rex," he yelled, "going to have a film tonight?"

"Yes, Lloyd, a real good Bible film."

He smiled. "I'll be seeing you. I'll be right in the front row."

Not thirty minutes later, little Lloyd did make it up to the front row—the front row before the throne of God. A careless driver didn't see the lad on his old bike, and Lloyd was rolled between the truck and the curb.

For Lloyd there were to be no more heartaches and sorrow, no more caring for a drunken father who didn't care for him, no more begging for work to get a few pennies for a bite to eat. He saw the Saviour he had accepted so recently, and for Lloyd, ". . . to live is Christ, and to die is gain" (Philippians 1:1).

12

Trust in the Lord with all thine heart; and lean not unto thine own understanding. In all thy ways acknowledge him, and he shall direct thy paths. Proverbs 3:5, 6

People in Chicago weren't interested in revival meetings, we had been told. But we found it necessary to stay in the vicinity in order to work out details for our new tent, so we decided to disregard the warnings. If one soul was reached, it would be worth our efforts.

We erected the tent on one of the main thoroughfares, and it was packed every night. People flocked to altar calls. Later, in talking with those who came forward, we learned that many of them had never heard the name of Jesus before! It seemed impossible, but older people — some in their seventies and eighties — came forward and prayed, admitting that they had never prayed before and wanted to learn how.

Chicago was a city ripe for the Lord. Necessity forced us to stay there, but God made the opportunity. And He gave us souls for His Kingdom.

Every time I built a platform for the tent and later helped tear it down, I knew there must be a better way to handle the situation. In my mind's eye I could see a beautiful trailer with sides that folded down to form a platform. It would be permanently wired for telephone lines to handle radio programs, and for electricity for lights and instruments. Now, with the new tent under construction, was the time to see if such a trailer was possible.

In Chicago, I consulted a trailer company and described what I had in mind: a platform-trailer van that could be wheeled in and made ready for services in minutes. On it we'd carry all of our instruments, which, by this time, included an organ, a piano, a harp, a vibraharp, cowbells and sleighbells, accordions, a bass fiddle, electric guitars, and other guitars—almost enough to fill the trailer. If we could, we also wanted to purchase another tractor, to pull the new trailer when it was completed. To our joy, the Lord provided the down payments for all this equipment. We dedicated it to Him and knew He would supply our needs each month when the payments were due.

Eleven schools, plus an extended trip through Alaska, had been Rex, Jr.'s schedule for his first school year. For the first year, it hadn't mattered much, we thought, but as we faced facts of further schooling, we knew we couldn't move him every seventeen days. We had to locate at some central point where Maude Aimee could stay with the children. Hot Springs seemed to be the logical place. My son would attend the same school I had attended, and my wife could continue to work for the Lord in the Gospel Temple, where my sister Ruth and her husband, Louis Davidson, were located.

When my family was comfortably settled, I rushed back to Gary, Indiana, to begin the next meeting. Those seventeen days apart seemed endless. We weren't used to being separated, and Maude Aimee was discovering that bearing full responsibility for two active little boys was more of a problem than she'd anticipated. They were good and tried to help, but . . . .

We returned to Arkansas after the Gary meeting and I was able to rejoin the family from time to time as we moved about the state. In the meantime, I wrestled with the problem of financing the new tent. Banks just weren't interested in lending money on a tent. It wasn't considered good collateral. What would a bank do with a repossessed tent?

I met with one defeat after another, until we answered Earl and Pauline Sexauer's invitation to participate in a month of meetings at their Oakland, California, Neighborhood Church in January of

1952. I hesitated at first—it seemed like a long, hard trip for just one month. But, when we took the matter to God, His answer was sure and simple: "Go."

One day I went into an Oakland bank to cash a check, and the friendliness of the teller inspired me to act on the spur of the moment.

"Who is the head of your loan department?" I asked.

The teller told me and pointed out his office.

"I'd like to borrow fifteen thousand dollars," I began.

The loan man nodded politely and asked, "What about security?"

I explained that our big tent was ready and we would have to give them a mortgage on it and obtain insurance, in order to get delivery.

The banker paused a moment, then said, "I think I can help you."

He dialed a number and asked, "Would you insure a tent?" After a short conversation he turned to me and explained, "That was a friend of mine—an insurance broker. He'll be right over to work out details."

I was in a complete daze while the banker and broker worked out the entire transaction. It seemed unbelievable. The insurance rates were half what I had been quoted by other firms, and the bank offered interest lower than any I'd ever heard of!

I came out of my fog to sign the necessary papers and, as I wrote "Rex Humbard," I realized that God had had a reason for saying, "Go to California." I had been stewing and fussing about financing the tent while God had it all arranged here in Oakland!

Our check was ready the next day and we sent it off promptly to the tent company.

Houston, Texas, was the spot picked for the debut of our "Gospel Big Top." The local papers published tremendous stories and huge crowds turned out. How do you put into words the thrill, the lump in the throat, the unbounding gratitude to God for the realization of years of hopes and dreams? Now, after thirty-three years, the "if only" of that thirteen-year-old Arkansas boy had come true. *Now,* "God had a tent like that." *Now,* God had "a crowd like that!" *Now,* we had a tent as big as the

Ringling Brothers — but our tent was a bigger tent in one big way. Ringling Brothers Big Top provides temporary entertainment; God provides words for life — the way of eternal salvation. The Gospel Big Top was a goal achieved, yet, in a larger sense, it was a beginning in a larger field of service.

As we moved on to Birmingham, Alabama, Dallas, and Oklahoma, the value of our new equipment was demonstrated again and again. School closed for the summer and Maude Aimee and the boys were able to join us.

We were in Kansas City when I received an invitation from the Reverend Paul Sorenson of Canton, Ohio. That seemed like a long way from Kansas City, but again the Lord advised us to go.

Canton *was* the place! Crowds turned out every night for a wonderful revival. About midway through the campaign, two newspaper reporters from Akron stopped at our tent by accident. They had intended to visit Meyers Lake Park, a resort in Canton that was featuring a famous name band, but once they were there, they stayed for the entire service. They saw for themselves what God was doing, and went back to Akron and turned out an article on us for the *Akron Beacon Journal.* Soon, people were driving the twenty-five miles from Akron to Canton every night.

As the closing nights of the meeting neared, I flew to Baltimore, Maryland, to check final preliminary arrangements for erection of the "Gospel Big Top." Baltimore had donated the use of the city park, an excellent location right on the Philadelphia highway, and ministers in that area were enthusiastic about sponsoring the services. All the plans were complete.

I flew back to the Akron-Canton airport where Wayne was waiting to meet me.

"Wayne, we're not going to Baltimore next."

"Why not? I thought everything was great there."

"It's strange, Wayne. I can't see any logical reason for not going to Baltimore. But somehow, I just don't feel right about it." We were both subdued for a few moments. Then I asked him, "How about driving me up toward the center of Akron?"

He wheeled the car around, and as we left the airport area, we passed the gigantic Rubber Bowl, Akron's famous stadium, and

Derby Downs, home of the world renowned Soap Box Derby.

An idea hit me. "Wayne, wouldn't it be terrific to set the tent up near Derby Downs? What a place for a meeting!"

"Derby Downs, Rex?" Wayne sounded shocked, but then he toyed with the idea. "Yeah, that's the place."

"Turn around. Let's find the man in charge."

Back at Akron Airport I met Shorty Fulton who welcomed us cordially. He had read the news story of the Humbards in the *Beacon Journal,* and he was impressed. In those moments I had complete assurance that Akron was where our next meeting was going to be. The tents were down, the trucks were packed; we were going to bring them to the Rubber Capital of the World— Akron, Ohio.

13

The Lord is good unto them that wait for him, to the soul that seeketh him. Lamentations 3:25

No spot in the United States is as hard to set up a tent in as Akron, Ohio. No city ordinances cover the erection of tents, so each individual request must be passed by the Akron City Council. In due time, the council sat and granted us permission to put up the Gospel Big Top on the selected site; we moved our tent in, opened the meeting, and began God's work.

When we opened, many people asked us to invite Kathryn Kuhlman as a guest speaker. Since we had also had many requests for Miss Kuhlman in Canton, I went to Pittsburgh to hear her myself. She so impressed me—in lifting burdens, saving souls, and healing bodies—that I invited her to join us at once.

Although I had seen the huge crowds in Pittsburgh, we were completely unprepared for the unbelievable hordes who poured out to hear her in Akron. She was scheduled to appear at the 11 A.M. Sunday service; by six in the morning I was unable to get into my own tent, which seated 6,000.

Twenty-five circles of people surrounded the tent on the outside, and we learned that over 1,500 people (who had attended our Saturday evening meeting) had spent the night in the tent in order to have choice seats for the Kuhlman meeting the next morning!

Newspapers estimated the audience that Sunday at 18,000.

87

The service began at 7:30 in the morning and lasted until 1:30 in the afternoon. Over 1,150 people knelt in the sawdust to pray and give their hearts to Jesus Christ. Kathryn Kuhlman was invited back the next Sunday morning, and again we saw a harvest of souls.

But before many days passed, local newspapers were carrying stories designed to damage the work we were trying to do. Wherever God is given free rein to work, wherever faith is great and God blesses abundantly, Satan tries to step in to defeat God's power for good. And Kathryn Kuhlman and our family had occasion to remember that corollary and to cling to Jesus' words: "Blessed are ye, when men shall revile you, and persecute you, and shall say all manner of evil against you falsely, for my sake. Rejoice, and be exceeding glad: for great is your reward in heaven: for so persecuted they the prophets which were before you" (Matthew 5:11, 12).

If opposition had come from the secular world, it would have been easier to bear. But it came from a minister who, in 1944, had invited the Humbards to appear as special guests in his church. He had greeted us warmly then, marveling publicly how wonderful it was to see an entire family working so hard for the Lord. But, in the intervening years, he had gone on record as opposing Kathryn Kuhlman's work. When she visited our tent, and hundreds of people flocked there to be saved, this minister suddenly changed his mind about the Humbards and tried to discredit us, as he had tried to discredit Kathryn Kuhlman. To the public, he let what appeared to be professional jealousy give way to "guilt by association." To the Akron papers, he vowed to "run us out of town."

Although our meeting had been set up so quickly that we had had no opportunity to get in touch with local churches to request sponsorship, the Akron Ministerial Association had had no objection to our meeting. (In Canton, twelve fundamental churches sponsored us; in Baltimore, a number of churches had volunteered to do so.) In contrast to this minister, the civic officials— Mayor Charles Slussor, Marvin Davis, the service director, and Russell Byrd, chairman of the city council—were very gracious. So a conflict with a local minister over what appeared to be a non-

88

Biblical issue brought me deep regret. I promised the Lord I'd not speak against him, for he remained in a position of a servant of the Lord; I committed the situation to God, praying that no souls would be hurt or prevented from finding Christ.

Days passed and a new logistics problem confronted me. Unfortunately, the tent's location added to traffic congestion and neighborhood commotion. We faced insufficient facilities to handle the enormous crowds attending the meetings, and neighbors in the area started to complain. I couldn't blame them. I'd had no idea such a situation would develop. The mayor called and said, regretfully, that he was forced to revoke our present permit, and all the Akron officials voiced their regret at having to take such an action.

But God had not yet told us where to go. We prayed earnestly, and we didn't have long to wait for His leading. A few days earlier, an influential real estate executive, O. Clare Conlan, had "hit the sawdust trail." For forty years he had been active at City Hall; he had been Potentate of the Shrine and had served on the Board of Directors of the Akron Automobile Association. Now, Mr. Conlan offered us his services. At his own suggestion, he visited the mayor to testify: "I've been saved at these meetings. The Humbards' ministry has done a great deal for me personally. I want them to stay in Akron."

The mayor took Mr. Conlan to a special council meeting and his testimony in that group turned the tide. The Akron City Council voted to let us erect our tent near Derby Downs. We could use the facilities of the Rubber Bowl which had no neighbors to be bothered by crowds.

This fulfillment of my dream that first day I stood with Wayne at the airport choked me up so I could only mumble, "Thank You, Lord, this is Your way."

The council suggested we move the tent by Monday, if it was possible. It was then Friday. We decided we could do even better than that with the help of the Lord. At the Friday evening service and on our late radio program that same day, we enlisted volunteers to help take down the tent that night and reerect it the following day. Hundreds of people responded. We worked all night and all the next day, and by the time the Saturday night service rolled around, the tent was standing imposingly at Derby Downs.

Normally, this task required at least four or five days of work. The electric company and other crews had declared it couldn't be done. We weren't the ones who made it possible—the Lord did. It was a testimony to God's power.

Originally, we planned a seventeen-day meeting, but that time was extended to five weeks. How could we cut off services while, daily, people demonstrated their eagerness to find Jesus Christ? During this five-week period, Kathryn Kuhlman returned for special services each Sunday morning, and all during the week, under our own ministry, we saw hundreds give their lives to the Lord.

The fruitful Akron meeting closed; the Gospel Big Top came down and we moved to Cleveland. But it didn't take long there to recognize familiar faces—the same ones we had seen in Akron. These people were driving thirty miles north to the Cleveland meetings. We might just as well have been back in Akron, for the majority of people came from there! A quiet voice told me over and over again that I had a purpose in Akron. I was not through in that Ohio city.

Three different suggestions were made about our immediate future. Dad Humbard felt we ought to take the tent to Florida for the winter. Clement wanted to go to California to conduct a series of meetings on the West Coast. I suggested we stay in Akron. I knew my idea was impractical, for Akron was too cold to continue tent meetings and the payments on it (as well as on the trucks and equipment) would continue through the winter.

I couldn't understand my burden for Akron, but I could not dislodge it. Wayne, too, felt God's leading and he urged that we stay despite the difficulties. In desperation, I investigated the possibility of renting a local theater. We were able to rent the Copley Theater (later called Copley Auditorium) for a six-month period for one thousand dollars a month. The auditorium seated almost a thousand and, from the very beginning, our meetings were crowded every night.

Maude Aimee and I decided that the cold weather made it imperative that we find a house, rather than use our little trailer.

90

We watched the ads; we put ads in the paper ourselves; we ran down every possible lead, but could find nothing to suit our needs. Then, one day, a woman called and said her neighbors were going to Florida for the winter and might rent their house to us. I hung on the phone with bated breath while she ran across the street to check. The neighbors let us have the place gladly—even with two lively little boys. God had provided once again.

A month after our opening at the Copley, Dad and Mom left for Arkansas. Soon afterwards, Clem took six weeks off. Wayne and I were kept jumping looking after the ever-increasing crowds attending the meetings. Our radio programs doubled—WAKR carried the Humbard program every night, in addition to our morning programs for them and for WCUE.

My sister Ruth and her husband, Louis Davidson, arrived to hold special revivals for us. Louis was an instant success with the Akron audience, and we persuaded them to extend their visit.

Suddenly, I was alone. God seemed to be making me preach and handle the other details as well, whether I liked it or not. Wayne was working on a temporary job in Cleveland while we held services in Copley Auditorium. Faithfully, he returned every night and each weekend for the services. Now, his employer invited Wayne and Leona to accompany him to Miami for a few weeks. Naturally, they felt it was a great opportunity, and we wanted them to take advantage of it.

That fateful month of December, 1952, was one I'll never forget. I started tossing in bed at night, my mind full of questions. Should I stay in Akron? Should I start a church and become a pastor? I couldn't believe what the Lord was saying to me.

I argued, "But Lord, I'm not a preacher. I'm more of a business manager. I just couldn't be a pastor of a congregation. I don't know how. But, Lord . . . whatever You want me to do. I want to win souls."

In the morning, I questioned my wife, "What do you think? How do you feel about staying in Akron?"

Maude Aimee didn't want to influence my decision. "Rex." she replied, "whatever you decide to do is all right with me. I want you to do God's will. Wherever you go, or whatever God wants you to do, will be all right with me."

91

The following night I was restless again. I found myself pleading with God. My whole life was bound up with the tent and our evangelistic work across the country. That was something I was capable of doing. Mom and Dad and Clement had left all the business details to me, and I didn't want to let them down.

Night after night, I felt like Jacob wrestling with the angel. Worn-out, and knowing I had to take time alone to commune with God—to know His perfect will—I decided not to schedule meetings during Christmas week.

That week I saved exclusively for the Lord. I took time to talk with Him. Finally, on Christmas Day, I prayed, "God, if this is what you want me to do, give me the answer through Your Word." My Bible fell open to Matthew 8:26: "And he saith unto them, Why are ye fearful, O ye of little faith? Then he arose, and rebuked the winds and the sea; and there was a great calm."

And a great calm came upon my heart. I had found my answer. I prayed, "Lord, forgive me for my lack of faith. Never let me be guilty of it again." Then I added, "Yes, Lord, I'll stay."

14

But without faith it is impossible to please him; for he that cometh to God must believe that he is, and that he is a rewarder of them that diligently seek him. Hebrews 11:6

When I answered the call of God and said, "Yes, Lord," that was only the beginning. He gave me a vision — a goal toward which to press. God left no doubt in my mind; I would be in Akron as long as I lived. I told the people the Lord was going to give us a great church. I knew that He would lead us, through our church services, to present the gospel by means of television to every state in the entire union. My decision was made. Now, it was up to the Lord.

My brother-in-law, Wayne Jones, was experiencing the admonition of God, also. He came to me and declared, "Rex, if you decide to stay in Akron, I'd like to stay too, if you'll have me. I'm certain the Lord wants me here."

After Wayne's return from Miami, his employer had offered him a permanent position with incredible possibilities; but Wayne was not to be deterred from his resolve for God. As far as financial arrangements were concerned, only the Lord knew what the future would bring; the position offered him would pay three times more than the best he could expect in the Lord's work. But tempting offers could not blot out the call of God he'd received the day he'd been saved.

With the assistance of my good friend Clare Conlan, I took out a charter under the State of Ohio and organized Calvary Temple,

93

Inc., in February of 1953. A few days later, when my family pulled out with the tent loaded onto the trucks, I stood there watching them go. I swallowed. Here I was with a church charter, no church members, and a little over fifty dollars in my pocket. Then I smiled, remembering it wasn't all I possessed! I had God, and a vision to reach the lost with the gospel. I had everything.

We started to look for a home for our new church. Copley Auditorium had been purchased by WAKR for a television studio, and we were notified that they would take possession on April 1, 1953, the day our lease expired.

I had to find a place immediately. I pulled the money from my pocket, counting it carefully — sixty-three dollars . . . sixty-four dollars . . . sixty-five dollars. That was all there was. What could we possibly get with assets of only sixty-five dollars? I was willing to rent some building temporarily, but nothing was available. We looked for land on which to build, but there was nothing we wanted or could afford. Next, we inquired about a building to buy. When we crossed the High Level Bridge (on the north side of Akron) into the city of Cuyahoga Falls, we noticed the Ohio Theater, situated prominently on State Road. It was big enough. It was in an excellent location. It had distinct possibilities. But the cost was prohibitive. They wanted sixty-five thousand dollars for a down payment — and I had sixty-five dollars!

Calling a meeting of our loyal friends in Akron, I asked for pledges for what each person would (or could) give within a three-month period. I had no idea of what building we could secure, but we had to have some idea of how much money we could expect. The pledges came in, and they were good. It gave me heart to press on.

Meanwhile, every conference I had with the owners of the Ohio Theater resulted in a reduction of price and terms. It surely looked as if God meant us to have the building. But the price they were asking and the price we could pay were still miles apart.

One day, when my wife and I were walking through the place looking around, Maude Aimee stopped at the side, with her hand on the wall. She was praying, "God, if this is the building you've picked out for us, help us to get it."

I checked the pledges again and I figured out the very best deal

94

I could make. I offered the theater owners five thousand dollars at the signing of the papers, another five thousand dollars the day we took possession, and five thousand dollars a month in payments for a year. (Later, we arranged to cut the monthly payments to two thousand dollars, for we realized that extensive remodeling would be necessary.)

Our friends scoffed and told me we hadn't a chance. They predicted the owners would never accept the offer. I just smiled. From a business standpoint it was hopeless, but I knew God was on our side.

To everyone's astonishment, the owners accepted immediately, and possession of the new Calvary Temple was arranged for in early March. The alterations were sketched out and we set to work, anticipating an opening date of April 5, 1953, on Easter Sunday. Maude Aimee was appointed official decorator, and it wasn't long before she was making arrangements about everything. I ordered a big, outdoor neon cross, forty-two feet high, so folks would be able to see the red and green lights from miles away. We wanted everyone to know this building was no longer a theater; it was a church dedicated to the winning of lost souls.

I was now pastor of what was becoming a large congregation. It was a tough job. In addition to working on our remodeling, I continued to broadcast three times a day and to preach at the services in our old auditorium. There was little opportunity to be alone with God.

One day I had my Bible balanced on the edge of the platform, trying to snatch a moment or two for study. Two workmen had just turned away, after consulting with me on some figures, when Clare Conlan strode up.

"What in the world are you doing? Back in World War II, I heard about 'Praise the Lord and Pass the Ammunition,' but I've never heard of 'Read the Bible and Pass the Hammer.'" He chuckled again as he saw more workmen head my way.

Even under the barrage of his friendly teasing, it was an effort to relinquish my former thoughts and catch his mood. "Clare, I've got to get some time for study. I keep thinking of all the days ahead, when these people will need to know the lessons God has promised to reveal to me as their leader."

95

Clare paused a second, thinking, and then his face brightened. "Rex, I've a trailer down in St. Petersburg, Florida, just waiting for you! Why don't you take time off and go down there? We can get along without you for a few days."

"That's the most generous offer you could make, Clare," I acknowledged and jabbed his shoulder affectionately. "I'm not going to be modest and refuse, because I'm depending on God to make me ready. I need time alone with Him, desperately."

I decided to persuade Maude Aimee to get away for a rest, also, but, when I broached the subject, she was firm in her refusal.

"Rex, I can't take the time. This week will be too short as it is. I've got to be here to keep the work moving. Go along by yourself, honey. We'll be all right."

She mounted a ladder and dangled some fabric from a rod, and I could see her decision was final.

A week before opening day we moved out of Copley Auditorium, and Maude Aimee drove me to the Cleveland Airport. The crisp March breeze was blowing as I waved good-bye.

The week in Florida rolled by more quickly than an Arkansas storm rips through a country field. Once more I found myself at the airport in Cleveland, this time returning home. I was eager to see the church. Before I left town, scaffolds were up, tools lying around, carpeting half laid—everything a general mess.

Maude Aimee greeted me warmly, and told me that people had worked all night the night before in order to finish last minute details, so I could see the church at ten o'clock that morning—but no sooner. I paced up and down, feeling caged. I wanted to go right down to see the church, but Maude Aimee insisted we give our loyal friends the time they'd requested.

In those two hours at home, I grew increasingly conscious of the sacrifice my wife had made. Her cold was worse; she seemed more tired than I had ever seen her. I was feeling fine. The time I'd spent in Florida was time shared with the Lord—time for studying, which had paid off in an increase of my faith. As a result of my time alone with God, I was rested, full of ideas for the future of this ministry.

Ten o'clock finally came. We pulled up outside the church and

I rushed for the entrance, anxious to look around. In the half-light of the new auditorium I paused, not able to say a word, not even able to control the tears. God had given me this wonderful church. "My cup runneth over," flashed through my mind.

Quietly, I made my way to the front of the auditorium and faced the pulpit — the place toward which God had been directing me. He'd trained me. He'd polished the rough edges. He'd made my heart tender and fixed upon me an overwhelming burden for the lost. This pulpit was my place of service.

Right then, I made some promises to God — vows I would never forget, vows that would guide me throughout my ministry. I promised I would give an altar call at every service held in Calvary Temple. I promised to pray fervently for our people, to follow the Lord's commands when they were sick and in trouble, to counsel them when I could help ease their load. I told the Lord that once need and financial burdens were met, I would never accumulate or hoard God's money. I vowed to reach out for new horizons, for there would always be work to be done. "Today is the day of the Lord," I repeated, and I promised to listen and try to follow the guidance of the Holy Spirit, both in my personal life and in my work for the Lord. We had a pact, the Lord and I. He had done His part and He promised He always would. I gave Him the pledge for a ministry centered in Jesus Christ, given over entirely to His glory.

I roamed over the newly decorated building. A few people were still working, cleaning up jobs that had to be done in time for open house that evening. They looked weary, but their eyes shone brightly.

Later that day, my wife and I acted as the official reception committee, greeting each person who entered the building — more than a thousand, before the evening was over. These were the people who had given their service to the Lord for the new church, and for this He had returned a double measure of His blessing.

Easter Sunday morning was a gray day. What began as a patter of rain turned into a downpour. Today was the day of our first Sunday school, and we'd been broadcasting that announcement, hoping and praying for a good crowd. We asked God for 1,000 in

Sunday school that morning, and God didn't let us down. When the roll was taken, the count came to exactly 1,027!

Because of her exhaustion and severe respiratory infection, Maude Aimee's voice had been reduced to a croak. When the Easter worship service started, her voice was completely gone. I walked toward the platform, tears streaming from my eyes, wondering how I could conduct the service. I called Maude Aimee to come forward for her solo, but she shook her head. She couldn't even talk, much less sing. I asked the audience to join me in prayer for her; then I placed my hand on her and prayed the Lord to heal her throat so she could sing for His glory. In an instant, God answered that prayer. The piano modulated into the introduction and she stepped to the microphone. Her bell-like tones soared out over the auditorium, as she sang the old favorite "We'll Talk It Over."

In the afternoon we had another service and the crowd appeared to be almost as large as the one in the morning. After the service ended, many people sat quietly, or visited in the lobby, remaining in order to be assured of good seats for the evening service ahead.

When seven o'clock rolled around, the auditorium—normally seating a thousand—was so packed that chairs were placed in every available free space, and still people were left standing.

I spoke to them simply, from a full heart. I told them how much I appreciated their efforts. Once again I repeated how thankful to God I was for all these blessings. I asked Maude Aimee to join me in our thanksgiving, but she was on the verge of tears, too touched to speak.

I smiled, trying to ease the strain. "Well, honey, at least tell them you're glad you married me."

She stepped to the pulpit. Her voice was choked with emotion as she testified, "Friends, I am glad I married Rex. We've had a wonderful marriage. Some of it has been hard, but we've always been happy. The Lord has been so good to us. I only hope God will continue to keep Rex as humble and thankful for God's blessings as he was this morning when he walked down the aisle with tears streaming down his face."

98

I put my arm around her and looked out over the congregation. Here was the work the Lord had entrusted to me. Then I added these words, "I can only praise the holy name of our Lord, for bringing us here to Akron to spend the rest of our lives, laboring for Him and for His glory."

15

But as we were allowed of God to be put in trust with the gospel, even so we speak; not as pleasing men, but God, which trieth our hearts.
Thessalonians 2:4

The Akron Beacon Journal ran a report of our new church's opening.

They've arrived — Rex Humbard and his family of musical evangelists . . . whose proposed advent into Cuyahoga Falls with Calvary Temple had been creating quite a stir, especially on State Road where he and his congregation purchased the old Ohio Theater to remodel it into a handsome church home. . . .

In the space of three short weeks . . . a prayer room has been made from the coal bin . . . the projection booth is now a radio broadcasting studio . . . and a photographic darkroom has replaced a tiny kitchen . . . Calvary Temple even has a special "bawl room" with cribs and baby accoutrements and a picture window overlooking the auditorium. . . .

So much had happened. We had incorporated the church on February 13, 1953, elected a board of trustees and secured a church home. Now, it was time to receive charter members. We announced that the church doors would be open throughout the month of April, and those who wished to join in membership that month would be listed as charter members. All who met at the cross of Jesus Christ as ransomed sinners saved by His grace, were welcome to our group.

People of all denominations had been praying for a revival in the city of Akron and, with that wide cross-section of denominations for background, the interdenominational ministry of our church was born. During the first thirty days of the initial ministry of Calvary Temple, over five hundred people became charter members. Crowds were so large that some sinners eager to find Christ, had to come back three or four times before they could get in the doors. We had no idea who had been turned away, but by God's mercy, many came back, and when they did, they responded to the invitation to find salvation in Christ Jesus.

Space for Sunday school became an immediate problem. We simply didn't have the facilities to handle the number that flocked to the church's educational program. The Lord led us to lease, for Sundays, the entire building of a large grade school twelve blocks away. At Grant School, the children could attend classes, leaving the Calvary Temple building for the adults.

Transportation was the next thing to consider. Eventually, every Sunday we leased twenty-two city buses from the Akron Transportation Company to pick up people in the city who had no way to get to church. The buses then transported the children from Calvary Temple to their Sunday-school classes and junior church in Grant School, returning them to Calvary Temple and their waiting parents at noon. Only a short time passed before Grant School was no longer large enough for the boys and girls enrolled, so we leased a brand-new school a bit farther away, Bolich Junior High.

Those early months brought tremendous blessing. Dr. O. E. Sprouell arrived from Tampa for our initial revival the first month, and he was followed by our old friend Dr. Glen Tingley of Birmingham, Alabama.

We began to organize the different aspects of a well-rounded church program — music, missions, youth programs, prayer groups. Very little time elapsed before we had an eighteen-piece orchestra and an enthusiastic choir, directed by Bill Everingham, a young man who devoted extraordinary time and energy to make the musical portion of the services inspiring.

The first missionary-emphasis service brought over a thousand people, with hundreds turned away. The entire offering from this meeting was sent to the foreign mission field, and this meeting began a very important part of our ministry.

We began to show Bible films for the young people on Friday nights; then we added illustrated sermons, acted out with costumes and scenery every Saturday night. These programs were attended enthusiastically by people of all ages, and they answered the question, "Where can a Christian go on Saturday night?" for dedicated young people throughout the city.

Under Wayne's instruction, the Adult Bible Class expanded rapidly, soon filling the auditorium completely. The church printing department turned out a monthly devotional publication, *Echoes from Calvary,* which was distributed widely in the area. A prayer room for meditation and counseling was open twenty-four hours a day, and visits and telephone calls from people all over Ohio were directed to this department. Prayer groups were organized under the leadership of the Reverend George Pryor, who also headed the visitation program. Shortly thereafter, more than thirty prayer groups had been organized in the city.

Programs featuring the Humbard family were being broadcast on numerous radio stations, and we added five television stations, as well. I preached every Sunday and didn't miss a service at the church for the next seven-and-a-half years.

Almost a year after Calvary Temple opened, I turned to Wayne and said, "The auditorium isn't large enough to hold these enormous crowds, Wayne. We're going to have our first anniversary soon. We've got to make plans to expand the seating facilities."

"How can it be done, Rex? This place has been ideal in every other way—plenty of parking, a central location. How can we possibly expand and retain the advantages we have?"

"I have no idea. But I've learned that when a person asks the Lord to guide him right, he won't make a wrong decision about anything—where to go, what job to take, what house to buy, what to do! No matter how big or how small the situation, if a man trusts Him, the Lord's not going to let him down."

"I believe that too, Rex, but expanding this building sure looks impossible right now."

"We'll trust God, Wayne—and listen every minute before we

102

decide—and then listen afterwards, too, for reassurance that we've heard Him right. He'll show us His instructions. God is never wrong. If we're on His side, that's all that counts."

The first anniversary of Calvary Temple came and went. The ministry was growing unbelievably. We'd put in what we called a "spiritual clinic"—a counseling service open from 10 A.M. until noon each day and manned by volunteers. Scores of people came daily for help. The results were tremendous.

We instituted a "Dial-a-Prayer" service for which we changed the recorded message each day. We had three radio programs daily, at 9:30 A.M., 10 P.M., and from 12:30 to 1:30, shortly after midnight. Response to the services had been so vigorous that we were feeding the church service, via television, to six TV stations in Ohio, Pennsylvania, and West Virginia, and we televised five days a week at 6:15 P.M., Monday through Friday.

Our outreach had grown—and not just by chance. It was because we were working! And the members could see clearly that I was pushing every bit as hard as they were. We shared the burden together.

I preached five times on Sundays at 8:30 A.M., again at 9:30 A.M., and a third time at the 11 o'clock worship service. I delivered a message for the afternoon service which began at 3 P.M., and finished up with the evening service at 7 o'clock. Unfortunately, this heavy schedule prevented me from knowing many parishioners and, with the children in public-school buildings, I lacked any opportunity to contact the younger ones, as I wished to do.

We had to make a decision; we *must* expand. We learned that we could enlarge the auditorium by "kicking out" both sides of the building and could add an educational building across the back of the church plant. But, before the final detailed sketches were returned from the architect's office, we'd already outgrown the building as we'd planned it—the building that would take us a year and a half to construct!

We looked around for another building to buy. Farther north on State Road was the attractive new State Theater—a building which seated 1,800. But, before we could conclude arrangements, we'd already passed the attendance mark we'd anticipated and we'd outgrown our plans for the State Theater, as well!

Weeks of prayer and consultation followed, and the conclusion was obvious. We would have to purchase a large block of ground and begin to build a large new church. With this in mind, we started to scour the local scene to see what was available.

There was some property at 2700 State Road that looked promising, but it was leased to a golf driving range. It was rumored that the owner was anxious to sell, but the Kosars—the lessees—refused to cancel their lease. I approached the owner and he quoted a price of $250,000. I knew that price was inflated so I made a counter offer. The owner remained firm—it was obvious from his manner that he was well aware of the recent publicity given us in the papers and of the rapid growth of our church, and he was determined to wring a quarter of a million dollars from "that rich church" for land worth less than half that amount. I gave up.

But God had other plans. The more I prayed for guidance, the more positive I became that the Lord wanted us to have that particular plot of ground. Finally, a Canton real estate broker friend, acting as a free agent, secured the property for $140,000 and turned it over to us. The broker was also able to buy up two adjacent blocks from individual owners.

The only stumbling block that remained was the Kosar brothers' lease. I went to Mike and Emil Kosar and laid our plans on the table. I asked them to figure out what they thought they would net from the driving range in the next eight years, and offered to pay them that amount. They agreed, and two days afterward, the *Akron Beacon Journal's* headline blazoned: CALVARY TEMPLE WILL BUILD THEIR NEW 'CATHEDRAL OF TOMORROW.'

Weeks passed in a flurry of activity. We sold church bonds, raised cash and, in less than ninety days, paid for the land and received title to the sixteen acres.

Shortly after that, a man offered the church two houses, situated on five acres, across the street from our building site, at the corner of Partage Trail. It was a tempting offer, but we had no money and the down payment alone was $5,357.

Then, a friend, who didn't attend our church services, counseled me. "You need that land to protect your future expansion," he said. "I'll give you $5,000 toward the purchase price, if your church will make up the difference."

I notified the congregation of his generous offer, and they promptly voted to pay the remaining $357. Dazed by the rapidity of the transaction, Wayne and I moved our respective families into the new church parsonages.

Now, we had ample land for future expansion—twenty-one acres in all. All we had to do was to begin. We had no fears, for man alone could never have accomplished these wonders. God was the answer, and we knew that He always would be there to guide us.

16

*That the trial of your faith, being much
more precious than of gold that perisheth, though
it be tried with fire, might be found unto praise
and honour and glory at the appearing of Jesus
Christ: Whom having not seen, ye love.* Peter
1:7, 8

Although we had the property, we were financially unable to start construction immediately. We faced the predicament
of providing space for services, so we put up a tent large enough
to seat several thousand on our new property. For the next two
months I held evangelistic services there five nights a week, and
continued to conduct our regular services.

Then God nudged me; it was time to get started with our building. I went first to New York, then west to Los Angeles, south to
Dallas, and north to Chicago, asking for a 40 to 50 percent
mortgage on our two and a half million dollar project. No one
would lend us the money.

The contractor who had built the shopping center across the
street from the church property offered to construct the church
for me and to obtain the financing. Mr. E. J. DeBartolo was one
of the largest contractors in the state of Ohio, but he discovered
to his dismay that he could get any amount of financing for a
shopping center, but none for a church. His disappointment
didn't hamper my faith.

I knew the trite old saying, "Where there's a will, there's a
way," and I added my own philosophy: "God helps those who
help themselves." And then I frosted the cake of my determina-

tion with the Biblical admonition, "Faith without works is dead."
I got going!

My original vision had been to build a big church, and through its ministry, take the gospel to every state in the Union, by means of coast-to-coast television. My church board was in complete agreement, but no one wanted to assume leadership in this project.

At a church business meeting, the congregation voted Rex Humbard head of the Architectural Committee; then Rex Humbard, Chairman of the Building Committee and the Finance Committee. Later they submitted the same name for spokesman of the Construction Committee. In essence, they were saying, "It's your idea. Go ahead!"

The architectural plans had to come first. I wanted a round building topped with a dome — to symbolize the world. Supporting this dome would be forty-eight pillars, representing the states which then comprised the union. I'd promised God that we would send the story of the redeeming grace of Jesus Christ in a worldwide missions program, so the structure of our church must speak of that goal.

No architect in Akron or Cleveland would agree to design a round building. "It's not practical," they objected. "You can't bend pipes; you angle them. Square corners are essential."

I flew to Chicago, and that afternoon, I described my concept of our new cathedral to A. L. Salzman and his three sons, all three of whom were graduates of the Architectural School of the University of Illinois.

As I described my vision, my words seemed to take wings. I told them the auditorium must seat 5,000; I told them about the dome; I told them about the pillars. I wound up my presentation simply, "Most of all, I need two things — plans for the building and sufficient financing. My dream is in your hands."

Mr. Salzman hung on my every syllable. When I finished, he turned to his sons and cried, "He's going to build this church and we're going to help him."

His sons were startled, but he brushed aside their questions and addressed me again. "Here's our deal, Reverend. We will design the building and help supervise the construction of it. We will be

107

paid the standard architectural fees." He paused here and looked at his sons significantly. "But we will ask for our money only after you are in your building, have secured the mortgage, and have the money to pay us—not a day before."

I was overcome. "Thank you for your confidence, Mr. Salzman," I stammered. "I've never . . . well . . . I don't know what to say. All I can think of is that God must have chosen you to help us."

The Salzmans kept their word. They didn't receive a cent until five years after the Cathedral of Tomorrow officially opened, but they never dunned me for one penny in all those years. I pray God will bless the Salzmans all their days for their sacrifice and good will.

As soon as I got back from Chicago, I worked hard preparing a show-and-tell presentation for the congregation. I used a broom, slides, and a projector to show exactly what the church would look like. There were sketches of the dome, sketches of the pillars, sketches of the Sunday school and sketches of everything else I could think of.

When I finished, Molly Kilbourne rose and walked down the aisle. Molly was an old, hunchbacked, needy widow, whom the church had helped out for some time, off and on. We took her groceries, helped her clean house, drove her to church, and generally did the odds and ends that her relatives might have done, had she had any.

By the time Molly reached the pulpit, tears were streaming down her cheeks. She could hardly talk, as she held out a quarter —the first twenty-five cents contributed toward the Cathedral of Tomorrow—and cried, "You're gonna' build it. This is all I've got to my name, but I'm gonna' help build it."

Molly has long since gone to her eternal rest, but that quarter was the symbolic widow's mite. Her faith, and the faith of the rest of the congregation (who were short of wordly goods but long on faith) built this cathedral.

I was unable to secure full financing, but I did manage to get a verbal commitment of a one-third turnkey mortgage—one-third payable, when we opened. I called a group of contractors together and asked them to carry this one-third until we opened.

I explained that I planned to sell church bonds for the other two-thirds, which I would then give to them as it was spent. (In other words, for each three dollars we spent, I would turn over two dollars to the contractors, and they would carry the extra dollar until we opened.) The contractors, like the Salzmans, agreed readily, and were ready to begin work at once.

I had the land; I had the plans; I had the labor—but I had no money! A friend offered to lend me twenty-five thousand dollars, so I flew back to Chicago on a Thursday and asked Mr. Salzman, "Could you start the job, if I give you twenty-five thousand dollars?"

Mr. Salzman's smile was sympathetic, but amused. "The circumference of the outer wall will be 943 feet," he explained. "For that money, the men couldn't even dig the holes, let alone pour the concrete and set in the steel."

I was desperate; I knew we *had* to get this church out of the talking stage, off the drafting boards—we just *had* to start building! "Well, couldn't you dig a little . . . pour a little . . . maybe put in a little steel? By the time you've done that I'm sure we'll have more money."

Mr. Salzman's sympathy overcame his amusement, and the next Monday morning, the Salzman Company's gigantic bulldozer and steam shovel began to dig a little hole—right in the center of a circle they staked out.

The *Beacon Journal* blazoned: CONSTRUCTION STARTED. Our own church members chanted joyously, "We've started to build our church," and they gave and bought bonds to help God's servant make that tiny hole bigger and bigger.

Together, Maude Aimee and I supervised the entire project. I let all the contracts for the construction, and Maude Aimee took charge of interior decorating and dovetailing many projects. Her high heels scampered up and down ladders to see that work was being done efficiently and on time, and she cajoled the workmen into doing what they'd never have done for me.

"How about staying with it for another hour?" she'd suggest, after crawling up to the dome. And they'd grin and keep going, weariness forgotten.

For two years I originated my three daily programs from the

109

cathedral site. In winter, I stood in the cold, wearing boots, gloves, hat and coat. In summer, I stood in the hot sun, describing progress of the building.

Those months were hard months — construction always is — but they were months characterized by faith. We saw daily miracles — big ones and small ones. Some people found Christ right in the midst of the plaster dust and lumber shavings; it was sacred ground.

God tried us in His fire. He refined us as gold. Only the vision of what He had promised kept us driving forward.

17

Being confident of this very thing, that he which hath begun a good work in you will perform it until the day of Jesus Christ. Philippians 1:6

Saturday, May 24, 1958 was the day sixty thousand people celebrated the opening of the Cathedral of Tomorrow.

In the morning, ten thousand gathered to view the March of Youth Parade which began at Calvary Temple and traversed the two miles up State Road to the new church. An airplane flew lazy figure eights overhead, trailing the banner, TONIGHT—THE CATHEDRAL OF TOMORROW. On every light post in Cuyahoga Falls and on Akron's Main Street were shields bearing crossed flags, announcing, WELCOME—OPENING, CATHEDRAL OF TO-MORROW.

The Radio Bible Club Assembly, six hundred strong, led the grand march. They were followed by floats carrying the Youth Band, floral designs of a huge Bible proudly proclaiming, ON THE MOVE FOR CHRIST, drum majors and the boys' baseball team.

When the marchers for Christ reached the Cathedral, they filled the cross-shaped concourse in front of the building. They knelt in prayer, and David Gibbs, Christian education director, asked the Lord's blessing upon the building and its worldwide ministry.

I stepped forward in the bright May sunshine to join in the dedication. "This building is a miracle—a miracle that could only happen in America, land of the free. And to God we give the glory."

In the afternoon I directed a tour televised by WAKR-TV and WJW-TV, which was fed to stations throughout Ohio, Pennsylvania, and West Virginia. All of the contractors and suppliers who had had a hand in the building were assembled, as I reviewed the construction wonders, mentioning details which had led Paul Metzler, art editor of the *Cleveland Plain Dealer,* to announce: "It is the wood engineering marvel of the century . . . the world's largest domed gathering place for religion, with a wood-domed canopy 4 inches thick and a vaulting span of 220 feet. In contrast to this, the second in size, the Cathedral of Florence in Italy, has a dome diameter of only about 138 feet."

We moved past the black-veined ebony granite entrance, crossed the lobby and entered the main auditorium. No interior supports marred the expanse of the 38,000-square-foot black dome. I heard murmured comments about the tear-drop chandeliers and the huge cross, measuring 100 feet in length — said to be the largest indoor cross in the world. As I pointed out that the cross was designed to reflect the moods of the programs; technicians demonstrated some of the more than sixty color combinations possible.

Then we moved down the aisles, between the 5,400 permanent seats, to the 168-foot stage, brightened by a red crushed velvet contour curtain. While the visitors exclaimed about the hydraulic lifts and remote controls, I was thinking about the real focus — the pulpit, and what it meant.

We went through the 200-bed nurseries, the chapels, the prayer room for counseling, the library, the 154 classrooms. I introduced my brother-in-law, Wayne Jones, as associate pastor, and presented the rest of the ministerial staff: George Pryor, Dave and Pearl Gibbs, the children's workers; Jackie Burris, supervisor of the missions program, and Will Chandler, the young people's director.

The first speaker was A. E. Salzman. He and his sons had brought their families, and they showed the building and spoke of our friendship with great pride.

A chuckle arose from the crowd when Mr. Salzman finished

his speech and his young grandson spoke up, "Grandpa who's the rabbi here?"

"Why, Rex is," Mr. Salzman replied and from that moment on, the lad's big brown eyes regarded me with awe.

Many others spoke of the grandeurs of the building that day. As they did, I kept wanting them all to see it as I saw it—not *just* as a magnificent building, but as a fountainhead for world evangelism. As the tour closed, I told them: "The Cathedral of Tomorrow was built by man, but it was created by God. I am not impressed with its grandeur. It isn't the building that's important. It's what's going on in it that's important—a worldwide program for God."

The official opening that night exceeded our greatest hopes. From West Virginia, Pennsylvania, New York and all parts of Ohio people arrived in cars, buses—even in trucks. Over 7,500 streamed inside, filling the building, crowded into nurseries, lining up in the halls. Thousands were turned away. And this was only opening night! For the next twelve nights I stood in that pulpit and preached the gospel of Jesus Christ, and saw those altars filled with hundreds wanting to give their lives to Christ.

I had prepared a simple salvation message—the story from the Gospels of the cleaning of the leper. I wanted those people to believe what that leper believed, when he looked at the Saviour and cried, ". . . If thou wilt, thou canst make me clean" (Mark 1:40). And by God's grace, this night they could find their sins forgiven—cleansed for eternity. As the service began, the fanfare sounded and the crowd grew silent. The klieg lights brightened; the cameras began to roll. The heat of the lights touched the pulpit, and I stepped forward.

For a moment I was speechless. Tears filled my eyes. And then I said, "Today . . . we've put God on Main Street."

18

I know thy works: behold, I have set before thee an open door, and no man can shut it: for thou hast a little strength, and hast kept word, and hast not denied my name. Revelation 3:8

But Satan is never idle. He had tried to thwart God's power when we first opened our Gospel Big Top in Akron. Now he tried again. Five and a half years ago we had had sixty-five dollars in cash and no members; on opening day, 10,000 turned out for the opening of our $2,100,000 Cathedral of Tomorrow. Naturally, there were many noses out of joint because we had grown so big, so fast.

As concern in the community grew, pressure was put on the contractors to withdraw from their contract. Fortunately for us, all of the contractors—Jews, Protestants, Catholics, and non-Christians alike—stood firm, except for two small subcontractors, with whom I had never had any dealings. These subcontractors proceeded to get mechanics' liens against us, which, of course, resulted in damaging publicity.

The main contractors weren't bothered by the adverse newspaper accounts; they bought out the subcontractors and told them, "Get out. You lied to the Reverend." But the publicity hurt us badly in the eyes of the general public and made it extremely difficult to secure the promised mortgage. Worst of all, it stirred up some of the church people who had bought bonds due in 1973. This group came to me and demanded their money back. It was only 1958 and I hadn't the money, so, for the first thirty days we were in the Cathedral, I sold $225,000 worth of bonds from the new pulpit, in order to pay what I could to this group who had bought bonds from the old pulpit of Calvary Temple.

We drifted along, paying the contractors whatever we could, until 1963, when my attorney said he could get the money, from a pension fund to pay them off entirely.

"Go get it," I told him. "I don't care where it comes from."

JIMMY LOVES REX, was one headline; BANKS REJECT HUMBARD, TEAMSTERS OK LOAN, was another. We got plenty of headlines and plenty of publicity—all of it bad. The papers bombarded me with questions: "Why did you accept a 16½ percent, fifteen-year loan for $1,200,000 from Hoffa?" "Why, with an estimated income of $60,000 a month, are you unable to stay solvent?"

I answered as simply and truthfully as I knew how:

> I accepted because banks have turned me down ever since we began to build. I accepted because this loan will consolidate our debts. Up until now, half of our monthly income has gone to pay former outstanding bills. We will repay the teamster loan for less than ten thousand dollars a month. I have been guilty only of raising money *publicly*—never once have I asked for a cent, privately. And this money, no matter what it's source, is for a good cause: To preach the gospel of Jesus Christ and to save souls. God is the answer.

It would take another book to tell you all of the miracles that have happened since the opening of the Cathedral of Tomorrow. All I have space for here is to give you the highlights of the last thirteen years.

On October 15, 1959, God blessed us with a baby daughter—Elizabeth, our first and only girl. And, on October 1, 1962, Charlie made his bow to the world. Like their two older brothers, Elizabeth and Charlie are healthy, happy children and a source of great joy to both Maude Aimee and me.

In December of 1959, our New Year's Eve Gospel Musical featured Mahalia Jackson.

115

In 1966, we purchased a twelve-passenger Lockheed *Lodestar* to carry our staff and instruments to TV rallies all over this country and Canada. Later, we replaced the *Lodestar* with a *Ventura,* and today we use a *Viscount* jet. We secured government financing for the Cathedral Apartments Building, and plans for 202 moderately priced apartments for retired senior citizens were drawn up.

In May of 1968, a model apartment was ready for inspection. Today, in addition to attractive apartments, this modern, non-profit project offers service-laundry rooms, elevator service, air conditioning, and carpeting.

That same month, we celebrated a double anniversary at the church — fifteen years as an incorporated church of Akron; ten as owners and occupants of the Cathedral of Tomorrow. In August, the associate pastors and their wives held a reception for our twenty-fifth wedding anniversary, and over 3,000 guests attended. Maude Aimee had to climb a ladder in order to cut the first piece of the beautiful 300 pound cake!

1968 also saw the realization of my dream of television coverage of all fifty states and coast to coast across Canada, and we had our first big rally in Toronto, Ontario, at the O'Keefe Auditorium over Labor Day.

A thirty-acre tract of land, three miles from the cathedral was purchased for a Youth Park. Baseball diamonds, horseshoe courts, and a large shelter house provide a well-supervised, scenic spot for youth to enjoy wholesome recreation. The shelter house also provides a dining and meeting area for various adult organizations — when we can chase the kids out!

Pat Boone testified to an overflow crowd at the Cathedral, in 1969. "This is one of the most thrilling moments of my life," he said.

Early in that same year, the Reverend Ron Hembree, Chaplain of Tucker State Prison Farm in Arkansas, and the Commissioner of Corrections, C. Robert Sarger, appeared on a Cathedral telecast to publicize the Farm's need of thirty thousand dollars to complete the chapel which was built by inmates, under the supervision of volunteers. I closed the program by asking each listener to contribute directly to the chapel fund.

In June, in response to a second plea from Ron, I went out to my native state to give two telecasts to benefit the Chapel Fund — in Little Rock and Hot Springs. One of the most rewarding experiences in my life was my visit to the prison. Ron greeted me from behind a table piled high with letters bearing postmarks that read like a travelogue — Oregon, Alabama, Iowa, Nova Scotia, Hawaii, Okinawa — six thousand in all. All six thousand were from my people, responding to the need of the prisoners.

Ron took me out to the prison grounds to see the shell of the chapel the prisoners called "The Isle of Hope in the Sea of Despair." I picked my way through the lumber, tools, and scurrying workmen to the front of the unfinished sanctuary, trying to imagine where the altar would be located. I stopped a passing workman and asked, "Are these round metal posts the ones that will support the altar rail?"

"Yes, sir. These are the same posts that used to surround the old electric chair — over the years, 176 men have been electrocuted right here!"

I stared at the man, aghast. How could they build a chapel on such a site? But then a thought hit me: what spot could be more appropriate? The posts that once surrounded death would now hold up life — eternal life for the lost and hopeless!

We crossed the road into the "Sea of Despair," where two hundred inmates were gathered to hear the visiting team from Akron. As the Cathedral Quartet filled the room with song, I moved about speaking to the prisoners. Many had a look of hopelessness in their eyes — the look of doom, or a death sentence.

But one, handsome, smiling young fellow stood up and called me forward. "Reverend Rex Humbard," he said, "we hereby give you an eternal life sentence . . . never to be eligible for parole, your maximum release date, eternity. We give you number 10662 — 10 for the Ten Commandments, 66 for the books of the Bible and 2 for the Old and New Testaments. Consider yourself a life member of Tucker."

It took me a few minutes to get the lump out of my throat.

Then I told those prisoners, "If I were to bring to Tucker the president of the United States, every congressman, every governor and every mayor of every city, and stand them beside you, what do you think the Lord would say?

" 'All have sinned—every one. . . .' Never feel that no one cares; six thousand people who wrote to Reverend Hembree care; *we* care; God cares. The Bible says, 'If we confess our sins, he is faithful and just to forgive us our sins, and to cleanse us from unrighteousness' (1 John 1:9).

"How many in this room will say, 'Rex, I need God's forgiveness and peace'?"

And many hands that had risen in revenge, hate, and murder lifted in surrender to God, the great Rehabilitator.

After the meetings in Hot Springs and Little Rock, we got the good news: the Chapel Fund had met its goal; offerings from our services had put them over the top! Not only would Tucker have a chapel, a larger prison farm in Cummins, Arkansas, would be able to start an "Isle of Hope in a Sea of Despair." God is the answer.

Each year, the Cathedral of Tomorrow has a challenge—a "Call to Action." At the beginning of the seventies, our challenge was to expand our missionary force of forty-seven missionaries in twenty-three areas of the world, and to extend our television preaching service to three hundred TV stations.

At the beginning of this decade, our New Year's Eve Special guest star was Pat Boone.

In March of 1970, we went to Hawaii, where we held three rallies during our three-week stay. We wanted to call personally on our many Hawaiian friends who watched us every week on three Hawaiian stations. When the altar call was given in Honolulu, the response was so great—over four hundred—that the crowd spilled over onto the stage, and tears of joy ran down my cheeks.

Later in the spring, a dedicated Christian who has been through the valley of despair many times shared her moving testimony with us at the cathedral—the Hollywood and television star, Dale Evans Rogers.

118

In Ottawa, we had to lock the doors of the National Arts Center to prevent overcrowding and, at the Owen Sound, Ontario, ice arena-auditorium, 4,000 people showed up for the 2,800 seats available—the overflow stood on the ice for the entire service!

In September, 1970, we attended the "Jubilee in Zion"—Illinois, that is—a town proud of its long and distinct Christian heritage. Over 5,000 people crowded the high-school gymnasium to attend our rally, and next day I was made "Honorary Mayor" of the town. While we were in Zion, we went to the Great Lakes Naval Station Hospital nearby and visited the Viet Nam veterans there.

It was an occasion I shall never forget. We saw many wounded men—very young men, most of them—and one we asked to look us up later. This young man, from Bowling Green, Kentucky, told me he had been in Bible School when he was drafted. He said he had watched me on television ever since he was a little boy —first with his family in Bowling Green, then in Springfield at Bible School, later on, when he was in training; and finally, when he returned from Viet Nam, in the hospital. While he was recuperating, he was finishing his training for the missionary field, and he had already been accepted by his Baptist Church Mission Board to serve in a foreign field.

"When you get ready to go into the mission field," I told him, "you let me know. You'll get some monthly support from the Cathedral of Tomorrow."

Late in 1970, we received our first publicity in a nationwide publication—*Parade, The Sunday Newspaper Magazine*. It was not the nationwide publicity that gratified me, it was the opening paragraph of the piece.

Which American TV program appears on the most stations? You might guess *Bonanza*. Or, perhaps, Johnny Carson's *Tonight* show. Wrong, both times. The program on the most stations, 242 of them in the U.S. and Canada, is Rex Humbard's show—an hour-long Sunday religious service that's formally known as the "Cathedral of Tomorrow."

We could have stopped with fifty TV stations and been completely out of debt, but that would have been misappropriating God's funds. We got the funds for television work, and I can't put it into a cold building—buildings don't preach. I'd rather have big mortgages and put the money into TV, missionaries, and publications to get the message out. If I could borrow a million dollars next week, I would, and just worry about the monthly payments. We'd make them somehow; we have never missed a monthly payment since 1963.

We may be condemned for big buildings, big business, and big debts, but no one can fault us for not obeying the great commission: ". . . Go ye into all the world, and preach the gospel to every creature" (Mark 16:15).

Periodicals and newspapers continued to give us publicity—some good, some bad, some middling. On February 1, 1971, *The Wall Street Journal* ran a front page story, with the headline: REX HUMBARD PREACHES OLD-FASHIONED RELIGION, USES MODERN METHODS. It was the first time I had ever seen a picture on the front page of this prestigious paper. I don't mind; I'd never have been there if I'd run a conservative church, and maybe the article will make some businessman tune in.

Time featured me as the "Electronic Evangelist," in the religious section of their May 17, 1971, issue. And I don't mind being called *that!* I am proud to be an electronic evangelist, for I believe that God has a plan—a plan to use electronics to get into the homes and hearts of mankind for Jesus. The only place we can have revival is in countries that have total religious liberty: the United States and Canada. And through TV, God is helping us blanket this area with His message. I feel the open door of opportunity for moral and spiritual reawakening—which could have impact on the whole world—in a short season before the return of Christ. But Christ will not come for a beaten-down, down trodden, defeated bunch of Christians. He will come only to ". . . a glorious church, not having spot, or wrinkle . . . without blemish" (Ephesians 5:27).

And, as my dad used to say, "Rex, the Lord's got a lot of washing and ironing to do before He gets here, if we're going to have a church without spot, without wrinkle, without blemish!"

This year is not yet over, but, it has already brought the realization of more dreams — more miracles in my life.

The Jerusalem Post ran a feature story, also headed ELECTRONIC EVANGELIST — and with good reason. While we were in the Holy Land, we filmed three videotapes which we plan to show on Easter, Good Friday, and Christmas; the latter tape shows young Elizabeth and Charlie at the holy sites.

On April 9, 1971, one of my most cherished dreams came true, and another phase of the ministry began. We purchased the facilities of Mackinac College along the shores of Lake Huron, on Mackinac Island, Michigan. The thirty-two acre campus, formerly owned and run by Moral Rearmament, is now known as the Rex Humbard Development Center.

At present, the center is being used for seminars and family vacations. Mornings are devoted to lectures, seminars, and discussions, and afternoons are free to enjoy the scenery in a horse-drawn surrey, swim, play tennis on one of the three paved courts, or golf on one of the two fine golf courses. Maude Aimee and I and the Cathedral Singers visit the center every Friday, so we can enjoy visiting with the families who are taking the "vacation with inspiration."

By September of 1972, we hope to have a full-fledged Christian college operative, with a thousand students, a chancellor, and a Christian faculty. We took over the license from the old Mackinac College, and our plans, right now, are to run the school on a cooperative basis — part-time study, part-time "cooperative education." This means employment of students in business and industry with college credit being granted for their experience. The part-time work will help students with their tuition, and for those who cannot afford any tuition, we hope to provide sponsors.

Sometime in the future, we hope to have a theological seminary, to be run on the cooperative work-study plan also — possibly two months in a church and thirty days in Israel. We would like to provide television training, using the cathedral equipment, a language school, and a pilot school for missionary pilots.

Train up a child in the way he should go: and when he is old, he will not depart from it.

In June, 1971, we took over the seventy-year lease on the Cascade Plaza from John W. Galbreath of Columbus, Ohio, for ten million dollars. Mr. Galbreath made it easy for us to buy this Akron property, because, he said, "If America is to survive, we've got to emphasize the old virtues of simple faith and concern for one another."

This purchase enables us to relieve the cramped quarters of our staff by relocating our executive and stewardship offices on the twenty-third floor of the Akron Center. In addition to office rentals from the center, income from air space will come to $20,000 each year. At the end of the lease period, the buildings will revert to the city of Akron, should they decide not to renew the lease.

As usual, I was accused of all sorts of ulterior motives. I don't know why so many people consider "profit" a dirty word; if profit is used solely for monetary motives it *is* a dirty word, but if profit is used for good purposes, it can accomplish miracles.

When I am accused of being materialistic, I often think of St. Paul. He made tents, you know, to support his ministry. I imagine if Paul were alive today, he'd be known as a good businessman, as well as an evangelist. In Paul's day, the church was the center of everything—the community, welfare, and social life, as well as spiritual life. He needed the tent money to support all of that. Who knows? Through our financial involvement, the Cathedral may feed more poor families than the welfare offices; we may curb or prevent more crime, through the gospel, than all of the police officers. In addition, we pay to the City of Akron over $110,000 in taxes on the Center Building alone each year.

I am not overly fond of statistics, but, like most people, I am not above using them to further my cause—the preaching of the gospel and the saving of souls. Here are some recent figures compiled by the Cathedral's staff, of which I am most proud:

We help support fifty-eight missionaries at home and abroad; nineteen are resident missionaries stationed outside of the United States and Canada; two pairs of evangelistic teams travel all over the world; one radio station in Africa covers a good portion of that huge continent; and one Christian college in the United States educates young people to carry on His work.

Our 1970 Television Rally Report estimates that we gave eighty-three out-of-town rallies which 155,288 attended, and 18,674 people reported that they found Christ at the altar.

Most important of all, as of September, 1971, the "Cathedral of Tomorrow" appears on 350 television stations every Sunday, at a cost of over $100,000 a week. The vast majority of people do not go to church, and the only way we can reach them is through TV. We must go into their homes—into their hearts—to bring them the gospel of Jesus Christ.

And, with God's help, we shall continue to expand our television ministry as fast as we are financially able.

Epilogue

If I were a superstitious person, I might say that the number "thirteen" is lucky, for a lot of the miracles in my life happened at thirteen-year intervals, or multiples thereof. Not all of them did, to be sure—one notable exception being my meeting and marriage to Maude Aimee!

I was thirteen years old that day in 1932, when I watched the Big Top go up, and vowed I'd "put God on Main Street."

Just thirteen years later, in 1945, my brother-in-law, Associate Pastor Wayne Jones, became a member of our staff. In 1958—again, the thirteen-year cycle—we opened the Cathedral of Tomorrow. Thirteen years later—in 1971—I realized two of my wildest dreams: the purchase of Mackinac College for the furtherance of Christian education, and tremendous expansion of our missionary and television outreach.

But I'm *not* superstitious. I know that none of these dreams—none of these miracles—could have been accomplished unless God had been leading me, guiding me, spurring me on for His greatness.

What will the next thirteen years bring, or the next twenty-six? 1984? 1997? I don't worry, because miracles happen every day and, with God's help, I shall continue to borrow and build, borrow and build, so that more souls can be born again in Jesus Christ.

This was the Lord's doing, and it is marvelous in our eyes (Mark 12:11).

125